Transforming FABRIC

30 Creative Ways to Paint, Dye, and Pattern Cloth

CAROLYN A. DAHL

kp krause publications
An F+W Publications Company

700 East State Street • Iola, WI 54990-0001
715-445-2214 • 888-457-2873
www.krause.com

Our toll-free number to place an order or obtain
a free catalog is (800) 258-0929.

Library of Congress Catalog Number: 2004100955

ISBN: 0-87349-616-7

Edited by: Nicole Gould
Designed by: Sandy Kent
Cover photo by: Mike McCormick
Detail of BLUE NORTHER COAT by Carolyn A. Dahl and Lisa Sharp.

Printed in the United States

Liability Disclaimer:

The author and publisher of this book bear no responsibility for any physical injury, destruction of
property, or any other loss, damage, liability, or claim resulting from the use of products and
procedures described in this book, whether used properly or improperly.
The information contained in this publication is presented in good faith and is reliable to the best
of our knowledge. No warranty is given, nor results guaranteed, since the conditions of use are beyond
our control. The author and publisher assume no responsibility for the use of this data.

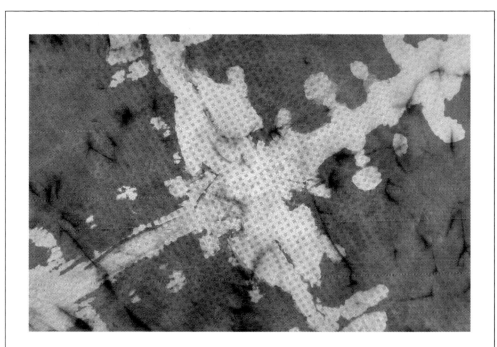

DEDICATION
To Thomas, Irene, Candace, Al, Chris, Aaron, and Brett

ACKNOWLEDGMENTS
I would like to thank Julie Stephani, book acquisitions editor at Krause Publications, for her enthusiastic response to this book and unwavering support in its publication. Further thanks to my editor Niki Gould, whose caring guidance moved the book seamlessly through all stages of production. My endless appreciation, however, goes to my husband Thomas Perry. Without his help in my everyday life, my creative life wouldn't have time to grow.

PHOTOGRAPHS
Unless otherwise credited, the photographs for this book were taken by Rick Wells, the artists, or the author.

TABLE OF CONTENTS

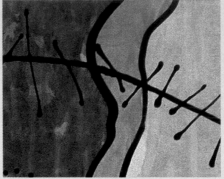

INTRODUCTION ~ 6

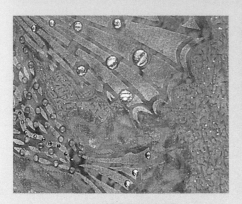

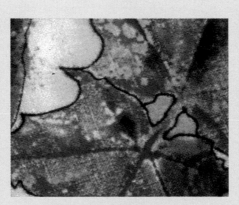

~ CHAPTER ONE ~

The Cloth: Bowing to the White

Cotton: Little Tree Lambs
Purchasing Cotton
Silk: Queen of Fabrics
Rayon: Artificial Silk
Preparing Fabric for Color

8

~ CHAPTER TWO ~

The Colorants

Early Textile Dyes
Modern Textile Colorants
Fiber-Reactive Dyes
Recipes for Fiber-Reactive Dyes
Frequently Asked Questions
Fabric Paints

20

~ CHAPTER THREE ~

Black-and-White Transformations

Five Good Beginner's Patterns

36

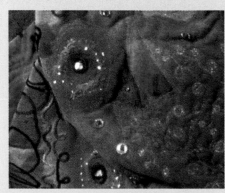

~ CHAPTER FOUR ~

Water Drop Patterns

Rain Cloth
Spray Cloth
Water Drop Yardage

42

~ CHAPTER FIVE ~

Nature's Patterns

Leaf Printing
Fish Printing and Gyotaku
Fish Print Stamps
Sun Printing (Heliotropic)

50

~ CHAPTER SIX ~

Sponge and Moldable Foam Printing

Animal/Sea Sponges
Cellulose Sponges
Synthetic Sponges
Moldable-Foam Printing

66

~ CHAPTER SEVEN ~

Compression Dyeing

Braiding

Twisting

Knotting

Binding

Scrunching

Folding and Pleating

Stitching

74

~ CHAPTER EIGHT ~

Heat-Transfer Dyes

Fabric-Transfer Ink Pads

Fabric-Transfer Crayons & Crayon Cloth

Transfer Pens and Portraits

Dye-Saturated Paper Sheets

Powdered Dispersed Dyes

86

~ CHAPTER NINE ~

Hand-Cut Stamps

Designing Your Stamp

Flexible Printing Plate

Sheet Foam

Erasers

Rubber Blocks

MagicStamp®

100

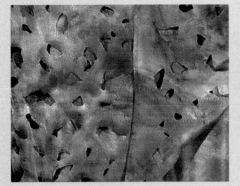

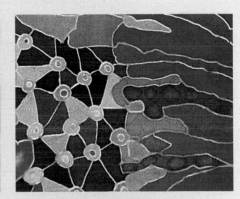

~ CHAPTER TEN ~

Destructive Patterns

Discharge / Bleach Patterns

Match the Fiber to the Discharge Agent

Devoré or Burn-Out Technique

110

~ CHAPTER ELEVEN ~

Wax Patterns

Dye Painting with Wax Resist

Planning the Design

Using the Tjanting Tool

Stretching the Fabric

Painting the Fabric

Setting the Dyes

Removing the Wax

Wax Stamping

Making Wax Stamps

Wax Stamping Procedure

122

~ CHAPTER TWELVE ~

Silk Painting

Silk Fabric

Gutta Resists

Painting Techniques

Salt Effects

Silk Painting with Pigments

140

CLOSING ~ 152

ABOUT THE AUTHOR ~ 153

FOOTNOTES ~ 154

SUPPLY SOURCES ~ 155

INDEX ~ 157

Introduction

EVERY TIME MY BRUSH TOUCHES WHITE CLOTH and floods it with brilliant color, a thrill runs through me. Even though I've dyed hundreds of yards of cloth and taught the techniques to others whose faces also light up when color seeps into fibers, I have never tired of the magic of dyeing and painting cloth.

It is that special moment, when not only the cloth but also the person is transformed, that made me want to write this book. I wanted more people to share my excitement, the beauty of my favorite techniques, the fascinating history and alchemy of dyes, and the wonderful in-process moments I experience as color transforms cloth. I've taught quilters, home sewers, needlepointers and embroidery enthusiasts, watercolor painters, basketmakers, weavers, interior decorators, teachers, and surface designers who all use the techniques in their own ways. But I want everyone to dye and paint cloth—to experience the pleasure of fabric filled with one's own spirit.

Many of these methods are timeless dye techniques whose creative patterns never go out of style; others are fabric painting or printing methods inspired by innovative, new products. For those techniques using dyes, all of the procedures, except for two chapters, focus on one type of dye: the fiber-reactives. Once you have learned the simple recipes for these permanent, versatile dyes, you can turn to any chapter in the book and complete the process confidently. You won't need to learn new dye formulas each time, or purchase more supplies, or change your workroom setup. Also, because all the methods are direct application techniques (the color is painted or printed onto the cloth instead of the cloth being immersed in a vat of dye), you can produce unique, personalized fabric in just an afternoon or a day, with either dyes or paints.

This book is organized into twelve chapters, each a mini-workshop focusing on a particular technique. Each chapter, however, is divided into additional methods and variations, so there are more than thirty techniques to fire your imagination. From free-form patterns to more planned designs, you can progress through the book, building skills and completing projects whether you are a beginner or an experienced surface design artist.

I believe that techniques have personalities, and it is important to understand the process from both a technical and a personal perspective. Thus, I begin each chapter with a story or observation from my experience or an interesting tidbit from history. These should help you select the method that matches the type of pattern or effect you want for your project. Then you simply follow the step-by-step instructions, complete with some of my tips and suggestions for successful results.

I would like this book to be a source book you can use for years. I have packed it with a wealth of ideas and photo examples to inspire you to experiment beyond the projects and processes presented. It is my hope that this book will become a worn and spotted-with-dye companion, with notes in the margin. However you use it, our mutual interest in cloth, paint, and dye will connect us. Your presence has been by my side from the moment the first words hit the paper until the last. Now as you read and use this book, my presence will be with you. Use it creatively, often, and bravely. Then spread the joy of transforming fabric to others.

CHAPTER ONE

The Cloth:
Bowing to the White

THE JAPANESE PHILOSOPHY OF NAIKAN suggests that we not only acknowledge the debts owed to people who have helped us, but also to the objects that serve us. Thus, before beginning work, a Japanese artist might bow in reverence to a beautiful brush or an office worker to a

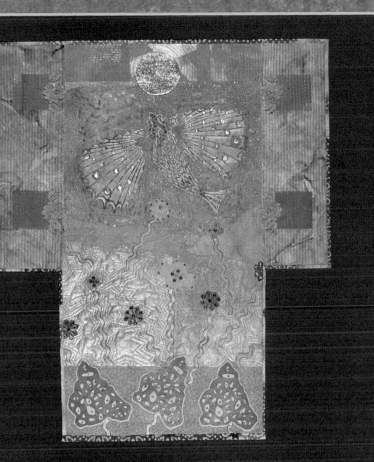

computer. Although I may not physically bow, I agree with the philosophy and am grateful for the materials that are my co-creators.

As a surface designer, my collaborators are the fabric, the dyes and paints, and the application tools. Cloth is perhaps the most important component. It is both the raw material that receives the colors and the final product that goes into the world to become something else. The most widely used natural fabrics for dyeing and painting are cotton, silk, and viscose rayon. These three give you a wide range of surfaces and weights and can be used with all of the techniques in this book, except the heat-transfer process which requires synthetic fabric or a blend.

When the fabric arrives in my studio, it is white, unadorned, ready for me to apply color. But I know that every yard contains the invisible fingerprints of growers, scientists, spinners, weavers, and shippers. Sometimes, when I unroll a bolt of silk from China, I can even smell the rooms it passed through. I will never know all the personal stories I'm rinsing away as I prepare the fabric for dyeing, but knowing a little of the fiber's origin and history makes me appreciate the cloth more.

above: FLYING FISH KIMONO QUILT by Carolyn A. Dahl. Cotton and silk, fiber-reactive dyes, Lumieré metallic paint, fish print stencil, sheet foam stamps, holographic disks from WTP, Inc. and quilting with Holoshimmer thread from Sulky® of America, Chinese longevity sign and eye of horus stamps © Uptown Design Co.
opposite page: Detail of FLYING FISH KIMONO QUILT.

COTTON: LITTLE TREE LAMBS

Cotton is the cloth of our land. The United States is second only to China in cotton production. Grown in our own Southern cotton belt, it's a homey, comforting fabric we've loved since we first slept under beautiful homemade quilts or snuggled into a corduroy jacket on a chilly autumn day. Long a part of our nation's history, we may even remember some facts from our childhood lessons: it is a relative of the hollyhock, it requires six months of warm weather, a cotton boll is the seed pod, cotton fibers can be $3/4$" to $1^1/2$" long, and Thomas Edison used cotton thread when he invented the light bulb. Later in life, we may notice that our food contains cottonseed oil, cattle are fed the hulls, paper and rayon are made from the short fibers (linters) clinging to the cotton seed, and folk singers immortalize the destructive boll weevil "just a-looking for a home" in a cotton field.

We've probably all used cotton fabric and perhaps even held a cotton boll in our hands. After all, cotton has been spun and woven for thousands of years. Cotton may even have played a part in Columbus' error. When he arrived in the New World, the natives presented him with cotton thread. As he believed that cotton existed only in India, he was sure this gift proved he had found a sea route to the Far East.[1]

Apparently, cotton had the ability to mislead a lot of early adventurers. In 1350, Sir John Mandeville returned to England after an expedition to India exclaiming over the sheep on branches he had seen. His exact words were: "There grew there a wonderful tree which bore tiny lambs on the endes of its branches. These branches were so pliable that they bent down to allow the lambs to feed when they are hungrie." As wool was the main fiber in those days, I suppose it was easy for Sir John to confuse an open fluffy cotton boll with a handful of wool fleece. Yet even today, the image of "tree lambs" persists in the German word for cotton, Baumwolle, which translates to "tree wool."[2]

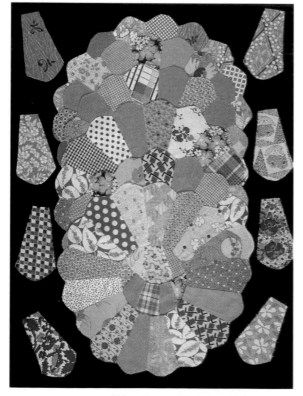

Old cotton quilt pieces survive as testaments to the beauty and durability of the fiber.

PURCHASING COTTON

When selecting cotton fabric for surface design, try to match the fabric's weave to your chosen technique. For example, if you want to produce detailed, precise images, you need a smooth, fine surface that won't interrupt your design. However, if your design is loose and free-form, a more textured fabric, such as corduroy, could add interest to a pattern.

The second factor is to avoid purchasing cotton that has any surface finish, such as permanent press; water-, stain-, or crease-resistant; or flame-proofed. Many of these finishes are resin coatings that are extremely difficult to remove without strong chemical scouring. Not only do these chemical additives block dye absorption, they may also weaken the cotton and hasten deterioration by sunlight.

One term you may find on the bolt label that is desirable, however, is mercerization. During this process, the fabric is treated with caustic soda (sodium hydroxide) while being stretched. This causes the twisted, dried cotton fiber to become smoother and more light-reflective.

The process was discovered when John Mercer, an English calico printer, filtered a lye solution through cotton cloth in 1844. Although the process sounds as if it would damage the fiber, he noted that the fabric became more absorbent, easier to dye, stronger, and less prone to shrinking.[3] Most important from a dyer's viewpoint, is that mercerized cotton will yield a 20% to 25% deeper color intensity than untreated cotton.

The reflective quality of the color in mercerized versus non-mercerized cotton will also be different. Non-mercerized cotton will not only dye lighter but will tend to have a matte appearance. Many people find this less-reflective, subdued quality quite beautiful. The colors have a mellow, seasoned look to them. Others, however, feel non-mercerized cotton gives their colors a lifeless quality. They prefer the mercerized cotton with its more reflective and lustrous surface appeal. It's all a matter of personal preference, but it is something you may want to consider when choosing cotton to dye.

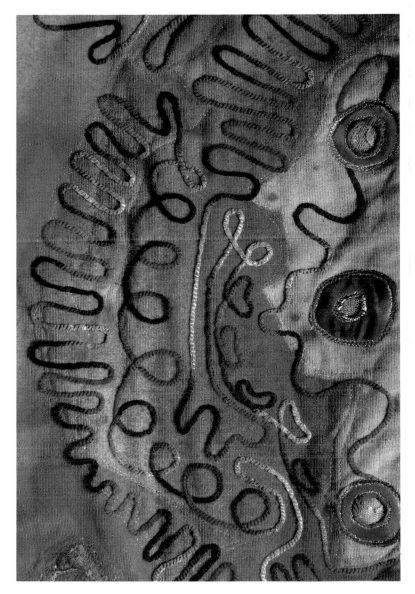

Cotton corduroy is a comfortable everyday fabric, but it can also be very luxurious and elegant once it has been spray-dyed and embellished with dyed cord and appliqués. Photo by Mike McCormick.

SILK: QUEEN OF FABRICS

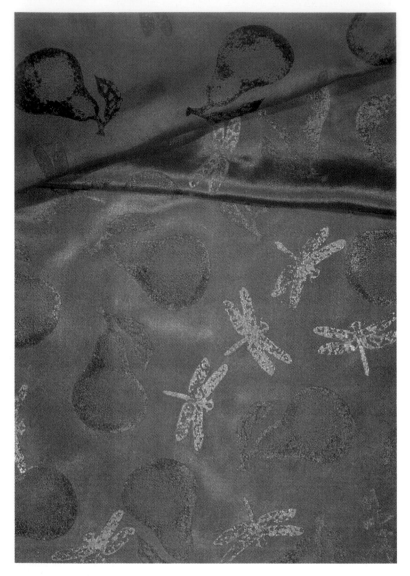

Once the color of white moth wings, this Thai Silks habotai fabric shimmers with dyed color and stamped images. Pear © Rubber Stampede, dragonfly © All Night Media, and Japanese artist signature stamp © Uptown Design Co.

Standing before an old crazy quilt, my eye zigzags through colors and stitches but suddenly halts. Before me is something that breaks the heart of every textile artist: a burgundy silk triangle crumbling away. Perhaps this sight, more than any other reason, has discouraged cloth lovers from using the queen of fabrics. Before rejecting silk as a fabric for quilts or fiber works, however, remember that many factors contributed to the deterioration of crazy quilt silk that now can be avoided.

Most of the silks used weren't new, but were often the best sections of someone's already worn out clothing—a favorite dress, a tie, or even a family christening gown. Already weakened through years of use, the silks were then stretched on an embroidery hoop and punctured with needles as the decorative stitches were added. Even though the silks were appliquéd to a background fabric, they seldom had the additional support that quilting or batting would have added. Often the layers were simply tied together. This construction method allowed the already fragile silk pieces to suffer more stretching and pulling during use.

When crazy quilts were made (approximately 1876 to 1930), their makers didn't know much about light damage or fabric preservation. Made as examples of a needleworker's skills, they were displayed on walls, over pianos, or as throws across chairs without any consideration of incoming light.

The greatest enemy of the crazy quilts, though, was the common practice of weighting silks excessively (also known as loading or dynamiting). To make a lightweight silk feel heavier and have a good drape, various types of fillers were added. The most damaging were the metallic salts. Black and dark colors, so popular in crazy quilts, often had the highest concentration. These salts did not wash out and eventually caused the fiber to become brittle and crack from the additional weight (silk can absorb more than its own weight of metallic salts). Mistakenly, people think the silk is rotting, when actually it is more resistant than cotton and other fabrics to the mildew and mold that cause rotting.

Luckily, the practice of heavily weighting silks is very rare today. If loading takes place, the law requires that the amounts be carefully controlled to prevent damage, or the silk must be labeled weighted silk. So if you purchase new silk and do not expose it to direct sunlight, you can avoid many of the problems now apparent in old quilts.

Silk is the longest, strongest, and most resilient of the natural fibers. Benjamin Franklin chose silk for his famous kite. Sky divers used to trust their lives to it as they hurled themselves out of airplanes in parachutes made mostly of silk. I hope quilters will trust it again for their quilts. After all, every fabric deteriorates in time, as does everything in life. We all want our works to last as long as possible, but sometimes we worry so much about the longevity of our objects that we forget they serve the quality of our lives.

The Divine Worm

Chinese empress Hsi-Ling-Shi probably thought that silk did come from heaven. According to legend, she was sitting under a mulberry tree when a silk cocoon splashed into her teacup. The hot liquid softened the cocoon, and a beautiful filament started to unwind. No tea leaves could have predicted what an important discovery the fourteen-year-old empress made that day, nor that China would hold the secret for 3000 years.

Today the methods of sericulture (the commercial production of silk cocoons), is well known by many countries. However, most of our silk still comes from the Orient, mainly China and Japan. America was involved in sericulture in the past, most notably by the Mormons and Shakers, but all that remains of the industry are a few mulberry trees on which the silkworms fed.

Two types of silk are produced today: silk from the cocoons of silkworms living in the wild and silk from cocoons of domesticated silkworms. The wild silk is difficult to dye (fabric paints work nicely though), and its coarser texture makes it less adaptable to surface design techniques, so our focus will be on the silk produced from the domesticated silkworm.

The creamy white Bombyx Mori moth produces the best cultivated silk. Once a wild silk moth, it has been domesticated for over five thousand years and is now extinct in the wild. Even though it has a long lineage, its own life cycle is short—about two months. During that time, however, it passes through four stages: egg, caterpillar, chrysalis, and adult moth (the scientific terms are ova, larva, pupa, and imago).[4] The story of its transformation is not only interesting, but also important to the understanding and appreciation of the fiber's characteristics.

Tiny Grains

The eggs, or grains, which have been kept in cold storage approximately six weeks after being laid, are bathed gently in warm water, dried in the air, and kept in incubators for approximately 30 days. In the old days, peasants who raised the silkworms in their homes kept the eggs warm by placing them under their pillows, in manure beds, behind stoves, or even in special pouches women wore against their breasts.[5]

The eggs are so tiny (pin head size) that 40,000 eggs weigh no more than a single ounce. No wonder two monks were able to steal the carefully guarded secret of sericulture from the Chinese in A.D. 552 by hiding the tiny eggs in the hollows of their walking sticks… at least that's how legend says the Emperor of Constantinople received them, and sericulture spread to the world.

Cultivated Caterpillars

When the eggs hatch, delicate white silkworms

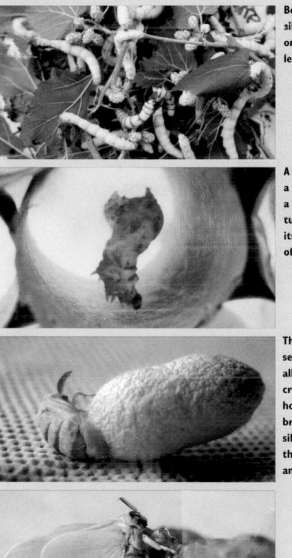

Sericulture

Beautiful white silkworms feast on mulberry leaves.

A silkworm spins a cocoon inside a cardboard tube, wrapping itself in a cloak of silk.

The silk moth secretes an alkaline liquid to create an escape hole, which breaks the long silk filaments of the cocoon. (left and below)

Home sericulture and photography by Connie Elliott.

about $1/16$" to $1/4$" long appear. Although they are caterpillars technically, they are always referred to as silkworms. Despite their tiny size (often picked up on the end of a painting brush), the little silkworms are ready to eat 10,000 times their initial weight. Although they will eat cabbage and lettuce, their favorite food is the leaves of the mulberry tree, which produces the highest quality of silk.

For the next three to four weeks, the only purpose of the silkworms is to eat, grow, sleep, and shed their skin four times. During this part of the growing cycle, the silkworms must be given careful attention. Their mulberry leaves should be crisp, cool, free of pollutants, and dry, as wet leaves will kill them. Their cages must be cleaned constantly and kept odor-free. According to some sources, Chinese women who tend the silkworms are not even allowed to wear makeup, smoke, or eat garlic. In fact, if the silkworms want to go on eating and refuse to construct cocoons at the proper time, the grower can use a plate of fried onions to make them lose their appetites and begin spinning cocoons.[6]

Above all, silkworms demand quiet. They must not be disturbed when sleeping or eating. According to folklore, a noisy thunderstorm could so upset the worms that they would immediately stop eating and fail to develop properly. So some poor soul was elected to go out into the lightning and rain with a live coal to drive away the evil spirits disturbing the worms.[7] It amuses me to imagine all the workers tiptoeing and whispering around the silkworms. I remember the little tree I had on my patio that was a host to another species of caterpillars one summer. The sound of them munching through the night kept me awake in my upstairs bedroom. How quiet can 300,000 silkworms be, chewing mulberry leaves at a rate of five feedings a day? Apparently, it's the alien nature of certain noises that disturbs them, just as the noise of gnawing caterpillars kept me awake.

Silken Cloaks

Soon the silkworms stop eating, turn a transparent pinkish flesh color, and begin to act restless. Having reached their full length of 3" to $3\frac{1}{2}$", they begin to search for an object on which to spin their cocoons. Once they begin bobbing their heads from side to side in a rearing motion, their caretakers know it is time to move the worms to individual cubicles.

As soon as the silkworm is placed in its compartment, it begins to wrap itself in a protective cocoon to initiate its metamorphosis into a chrysalis. Working in a figure eight pattern, the worm ejects two filaments from a hole in its lower jaw, called the spinneret. One filament is a barely visible protein filament called fibroin, the other a glutinous substance called sericin, or silk gum. The two filaments merge and harden when they reach the air.

Within 24 hours, the worm is hidden from view, but continues to spin inside the cocoon for three to four days. It is estimated that the caterpillar spins 20 to 30 layers of filaments or approximately 1,000 to 4,000 feet of unbroken filament. As it gets tired, the fibers at the center of cocoon will be weaker. Finally exhausted, the silkworm rests, wrapped in its silken cloak. The cocoon must not be disturbed as the transformation inside takes place.

Chrysalis Dreams

In about eight days, the silkworm will have remade itself inside and out. Shedding its caterpillar skin, it becomes a brown shell filled with yellow liquid (the chrysalis), which develops into an adult moth. If the moth were allowed to emerge, however, the long filament of the cocoon would be broken into short threads where the moth escaped.

In home-raised cocoons, where the silk production is small, the cocoon can be unreeled when freshly spun with the live chrysalis remaining inside. Some silk filament is allowed to remain around the chrysalis, so it can grow into a moth and emerge unharmed. In large scale silk production, however, the cocoons will be stored before unwinding the silk, so the chrysalis development must be halted with heat or steam. Having a tender heart, I like to think the chrysalis is merely sleeping, dreaming of flowers, colors, and flight.

White Moths

Out of each batch, some cocoons, often called queen cocoons regardless of sex, must be allowed to mature and produce the next generation. Since some of each sex must be collected, the cocoons are sorted by weight (the females are heavier than the males). When the creamy white moths emerge, they unfold their useless wings and mate. The female lays anywhere from 300 to 600 eggs and dies within a week.

Unlike a butterfly that has a proboscis to take in nectar and water, the silk moth has no means of nourishment. It does not have a digestive system and cannot drink or chew. Perhaps that is why the silkworm's appetite is so voracious. It must store nutrients to be passed along to the moth so it can survive long enough to complete its short life cycle.[8]

Divine Threads

When they are ready to be unwound, the cocoons are placed in hot water to soften the sericin (glue) so the beginning of the silk filament can be found. Because the strand is so delicate, the filaments of five or six cocoons are unwound together onto one bobbin. Even this many cocoons produce a very fine strand. To make a more usable thread, six or seven bobbins must be twisted together, the number depending on the type of silk to be woven. When you realize that it takes about 110 cocoons for the silk in one man's tie and 1500 for a dress, perhaps you understand why silk fabric is so precious.

To make one silk dress, 1500 silk cocoons are needed. PUZZLE DRESS by Carolyn A. Dahl. Spray-dyed silk with puzzle pieces as masks.

RAYON: ARTIFICIAL SILK

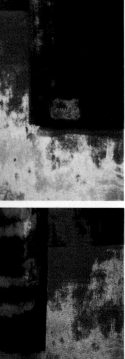

Once called artificial silk, rayon was renamed because it reflected the sun's rays. Rayon velvet dyed with fiber-reactive dyes.

Rayon was developed as a silk substitute by a Frenchman. When a disease threatened to destroy whole colonies of European silkworms, Louis Pasteur was hired in 1878 to solve the mystery of the black and dying worms. A pupil of his, a Frenchman named Count Hilaire de Chardonnet, was also studying the silkworms.[9]

Perhaps because he believed that the whole silk industry was on the brink of extinction, Chardonnet hoped to duplicate the silkworm's product using chemicals. After all, silk wasn't really a fiber, but a secretion. The secretion took the shape of a filament when the worm forced the liquid through a hole, or spinneret. Once out of the silkworm's body, the shaped secretion hardened in the air. Chardonnet knew that a spinneret could be mimicked in metal, but finding the right chemical combination to duplicate the secretion was more difficult.

In 1884, Chardonnet succeeded by dissolving nitrocellulose in alcohol and ether. He opened a factory to produce artificial silk, which it was called for many years. In 1924, it was given a new name, rayon, because it described the early, lustrous, almost metallic fabric as it reflected the sun's rays.

Chardonnet is credited as the inventor of rayon, the first man-made fiber. But he really should share the honor with the silkworm who was the source for the idea. Chardonnet admitted he had never really reproduced the silkworm's product, but he did introduce a new fiber to the world. Over the years, the processes for producing rayon have changed greatly, and today's buyer can select lustrous fabrics that resemble silk, dull rayons that mimic cotton, sheers that look like chiffon, or rayons as heavy as satins. Mixed with other fibers, rayon has come into its own and finally out of the shadow of silk.

Purchasing Rayon for Dyeing

There are two types of rayon—viscose rayon, which the fiber-reactive dyes used in this book will dye, and acetate rayon, which they will not. Both rayons come from cellulosic materials (wood pulp or cotton linters) but are processed differently. Viscose rayon is produced through an alkali process; it receives its name because the resulting solution is thick like honey. It is then forced through a metal spinneret and extruded as a fiber. Acetate rayon is produced by an acid process, specifically acetic acid, for which it is named.

Unfortunately, the labels on fabric bolts do not always identify whether the rayon is viscose or acetate. If you order your fabric from a dye supplier, you will always get the dyeable rayon. If you purchase your fabric elsewhere, ask for a small sample. Take it home and give it the burn test. Viscose rayon will produce a feathery ash that smells like burnt paper. Acetate rayon will leave a charred, bead-like residue that has a slight vinegar smell (the acetic acid in its process).

Whether you choose to work with tree lambs, the divine worm, or the sun's rays, try to develop a respect for the fiber. Cloth isn't just woven threads. Like the incense fragrance that remains in the textiles I bought in a Mexican market years ago, each piece of fabric you use has a history clinging to its fibers. It came from a plant, an animal, a worm, or a synthetic solution. Years of industrial inventions, scientific research, and loving care were required to bring it to you. I think it's worth a little bow of recognition.

PREPARING FABRIC FOR COLOR

Even if you've purchased fabrics free of specific surface treatments, they will still contain some type of sizing added for consumer appeal. To remove these additives and any other impurities, the fabrics must be thoroughly hand or machine washed before coloring.

As the fabric will shrink during the washing process, always allow 1" to 2" extra per yard. However, after a silk pongee lost 3" per yard during washing, I now do a test sample first whenever I have limited yardage or am working on a commission.

Whatever your fabric, add neither fabric softener to the wash, nor fabric softener sheets to the dryer. Your purpose in washing the fabric is to remove, and avoid adding, any chemicals that may interfere with the colorant's bonding with the fiber.

Washing Cotton

Cotton is a very durable fabric (the Army uses it for their uniforms) and can withstand machine agitation and high temperatures as its fibers are stronger wet than dry. Machine wash cotton in hot water, with a laundry detergent or a commercial scouring agent like Synthrapol (2 tsp. Synthrapol SP and 2 tsp. Pro Dye Activator per gallon of wash water (140-200 degrees F). Rinse cotton and machine dry at regular setting.

Iron fabric at a cotton setting, using steam if necessary. Cotton is not as elastic as other natural fibers and wrinkles considerably after the sizing has been removed during washing. Wrinkles can interfere with some patterning processes and block dye penetration, so they should be removed as completely as possible.

If you do not intend to use your fabric right away, store it in a light, airy spot to avoid mildew. Although cotton fabric with sizing in it is more susceptible, mildew can form on clean fiber also. Mildew is a parasitic fungus that changes cellulose to sugar, on which it then feeds. As cotton is 85 to 90 percent cellulose and absorbs moisture quickly but dries slowly, it is very prone to the fungus.

Washing Silk

For years, I hand washed all my silk, until a banquet-size tablecloth changed my mind. Usually I

FLORAL TABLECLOTH by Carolyn A. Dahl. Dye painting with wax resist.

wash the silk as yardage, paint the design, and then have the pieces seamed together later. But a clever interior designer wanted the large floral pattern I was to paint to cross over the seams and arrived with the tablecloth completely constructed—all 20 yards.

As the silk could not be taken apart again, but did have to be washed before painting, I tried to solve the problem as best I could. Lacking a large sink, I chose my biggest plastic garbage can, my garden hose, and a bare patch in my backyard. After carrying buckets of hot water from the house and filling the container with additional hose water, I plunged the lightweight silk into the sudsy water.

At the first swish, I knew I was in trouble. Dry silk that may only weigh a pound suddenly becomes about five pounds when wet. My grand plan had been to wash, tilt the can to drain off

NUCLEAR FOREST #2 by Carolyn A. Dahl. Fiber-reactive dyes on silk, compression and discharge techniques.

soapy water, refill with hose water, and repeat until totally rinsed. However, just moving the silk in the water was like lifting boulders.

Once started, however, I had no choice but to continue my ill-fated procedure. After a long time of tugging, pushing, and pounding on the silk lump in the soapy water, I started to tilt the can to let some of the water slosh out. I braced one foot on the can's bottom and held on to the can's lip with both hands as I tilted the container. The water moved to the edge. All seemed well. But then the dye devils arrived. Suddenly the flexible plastic started stretching. I pulled frantically in the opposite direction of the pouring water, but the can only elongated more. The balance of power shifted and the wet silk slid quickly over the lid and into the dirt. I followed, tumbling over the can and landing on the silk in a rush of water.

Machine Washing Silk

Since that experience, I have washed every type of silk in my machine (except for raw silk). I avoid soaps or detergents that contain alkalies, as even weak alkalies such as borax, ammonia, and phosphate of soda can deteriorate the fiber and diminish luster.[10] (When the silk moth is ready to emerge from its cocoon, it excretes an alkaline liquid to dissolve the silk filaments and create its escape hole. So take a clue from nature.) Neutral, non-alkaline dish washing soaps, such as clear Ivory Liquid, work well. Never use chlorine bleach on silk.

Use a delicate cycle (silk fiber is weaker when wet but returns to its original strength when dry), with a non-alkaline soap, lukewarm water, and a cool water rinse to minimize wrinkles. Many people subject their silks to higher temperatures and more vigorous washing than I do. Although the silks will survive, I feel they lose some of their spirit and luster.

Either line dry the silk away from sunlight or iron it dry. I prefer to iron the fabric while wet or very damp, when the wrinkles are easy to remove. If you are unable to do so immediately, keep the wet silk rolled up in a terry cloth towel and store it in the refrigerator.

Washing Rayon

If your rayon is lightweight or sheer, follow the

silk washing instructions. Otherwise rayon can be washed with the same procedure as cotton.

Ready-to Dye-Fabric

Instead of washing and desizing the fabric yourself, you can purchase prepared-for-dyeing (PFD) fabrics that are ready to paint or dye. These fabrics are especially helpful when you're working with large quantities of fabric and would rather spend your time painting than preparing.

Detail of NUCLEAR FOREST #2 by Carolyn A. Dahl.

CHAPTER TWO

The Colorants

WHEN YOU DECIDE TO DYE OR PAINT YOUR OWN FABRICS, you become part of an ancient tradition. The desire for colored cloth seems to have touched every century and country. Few of the early textiles have survived except as time-worn fragments. Even less remains to remind us of the early dyers—a street name in Florence, Italy (Corso de' Tintori), a mention in Chaucer's THE CANTERBURY TALES, or a fading recipe book in some museum archive. Most of the time, we have to create a picture of our craft ancestors from a few good historical details and a lot of imagination.

From everything I've ever read about early dyers, I'm sure that they were very clever, observant, and inventive. They studied nature closely. They knew which berries stained, what leaf pounded into cloth would leave a chlorophyll imprint, and how that imprint could change colors if it were soaked in a certain stream, in sea water, or buried in wood ashes.

Not only were their discoveries important to the coloring of cloth, but also to other early professions. As many natural dyes were medicines, the dyers' skill in identifying and cultivating the plants was instrumental to the development of a more scientific approach to healing. Painters, too, owe their knowledge of many pigments to the dyers' early notebooks.

UNDERWATER by Carolyn A. Dahl. Detail of the silk work showing how fabric paint can be used thick or thin. Photo by Mike McCormick

EARLY TEXTILE DYES

Because it often took years of experimentation to develop reliable recipes, early dyers were secretive and superstitious. Workers signed oaths and were threatened if they revealed any part of the process. Only a select few knew the recipes kept in carefully guarded notebooks. Outsiders were definitely unwelcome and discouraged from visiting the dye houses by rumors of terrifying apparitions that haunted the premises.

Some cultures wouldn't allow "mean spirited" people to tend the dye pot in case their bad attitude might affect the dye's success. In Japan, sake is still offered to the Indigo dye pot because the dye is believed to be a living substance. Many groups honored dye gods such as Melkarth, the Phoenician god whose sheep dog is supposed to have bitten a shellfish and discovered the color purple from his stained jaws.[1] Even modern day dyers agree that it doesn't hurt to have a dye goddess hovering around the studio or to throw a good luck penny into the steamer pot before the fabric meets the heat.

As secretive and superstitious as the early dyers were, they probably didn't need to worry much about visitors. Only the most determined spy would have come near a dye house. As much as everyone admired their products, no one wanted to be their neighbors. The dyers' trade was considered a dirty, unclean occupation best exiled to the outskirts of town, next to the equally smelly tanners. You can't blame the townspeople when you think about some of the dye sources (insects, shellfish glands, algae) and extraction methods (boiling, salting, fermenting in urine).

The most difficult color to obtain was purple. According to Gosta Sandberg[2], the raw material for the purple dye was found in mollusks that divers collected at the bottom of the Mediterranean sea. The piles of crushed shells, many layers deep (12,000 mollusks yield a small amount of dye), have helped historians pinpoint the locations of the old dye houses along the Mediterranean. Even some old shellfish dyed textiles can be identified because of the slightly fishy smell clinging to their fibers. It may also explain why the aristocrats draped in their luxurious purple garments always wore copious amounts of perfume.

Perhaps it's not strange that the revolution in dyeing methods in 1856 would be connected to the color purple. Maybe eighteen-year-old William Henry Perkin was thinking of purple's preciousness when his search for synthetic quinine produced only a dark precipitate.[3] Why else would he have dipped a piece of silk into it and discovered the first synthetic dye—mauve? Although his new coal tar derivative dye wasn't very colorfast, it was used immediately and stimulated more dye research. Scientists reasoned that if the difficult light purple could be produced in a laboratory, so could other colors. Returning to the natural dye sources one last time, they isolated and analyzed the coloring agents in each and began to reproduce them chemically. Soon other synthetic dyes followed in rapid succession: 1875, acid dyes; 1880, original azoic dyes; 1901, vat dyes; 1915, metal-complex dyes; 1923, disperse dyes; and in 1956 reactive dyes.[4]

The dyer's life had become easier but totally transformed. Suddenly a lifetime of natural dyeing knowledge was obsolete. Unusual and rare plants no longer had a function and disappeared. Certain colors became lost to our eyes and can never be duplicated again. Not only had the source for the colors changed but also the connection. In natural dyeing, the object from which the colorant is drawn usually has a beauty of its own, but with synthetic dyes and paints, as Manilo Brusatin says, the color "transcends the substances from which they are derived...beautiful colors thro artifice."[5]

Modern Textile Colorants

Today's textile coloring agents are divided into two categories: dyes and paints. The main difference to remember is that dyes can be made to dissolve in water and react with the fiber, either by chemically bonding or by coating. They become part of the fiber and cannot be felt on the fabric's surface. Fabric paints contain solid pigment particles, nonreactive and insoluble in water, that must adhere to the fabric. As they do not penetrate the fiber but lie on the fabric's surface, a very slight texture can be felt due to the binder, which glues them to the fabric. The techniques in this book are all direct application techniques (colorant is applied to the fabric's surface instead of immersing the fabric in a container of dye) and thus either dye or paint can be used if some modifications are made to the process.

Lumieré metallic fabric paints on cotton. Stamps: Chinese longevity sign and eye of horus © Uptown Design Inc. Photo by Mike McCormick.

FIBER-REACTIVE DYES

The dyeing techniques in this book will use fiber-reactive dye (this is its dye class name, but it is sold under different brand names such as Procion® or Sabracron®). I have used these dyes for years because they adapt to many techniques, offer a large range of permanent colors, and don't require toxic chemicals. Although I do use other dyes for some projects, and invite you to experiment with all the ones on the market, I still return to fiber-reactives for most of my work.

First developed in 1956 by ICI (Imperial Chemical Industries, Ltd.), fiber-reactive dyes are derived from petrochemicals. Although synthetic dyes, they will not color synthetic fabric. The fibers they will dye are all natural: cotton, silk, viscose rayon, linen. Wool can be dyed but requires special treatment and heat. Fiber-reactive dyes are very permanent as the fiber molecule chemically bonds (or reacts) with the dye molecule. The information in this book is for Procion® fiber-reactive dyes, the MX and H series. If you are using another brand, check the manufacturer's instructions for differences.

Procion® MX Series

The basic procedure for all fiber-reactive dyes is to mix the colors in chemical water (see page 25); add an alkali activator, either baking soda (bicarbonate of soda) or soda ash (sodium carbonate, washing soda, fixer) to start the chemical reaction; apply the dye; and later set the fabric to make the colors permanent. However, you do have a choice as to whether you want to use the MX series, which reacts quickly, or the slower reacting H series.

If you only want to stock one dye, the MX series would be a good choice as you can use it both for immersion dyeing (one-color dye bath) and for direct application techniques (applying colors by painting, stamping, etc.). The dye comes in powders with approximately 110 colors from which to choose (the dye powder will last up to three years if stored in a dry, cool environment).

The MX series is a very reactive dye, meaning that the minute it gets wet it begins to change chemically and bond with the water. For this reason, it isn't sold in liquid form like the H series.

Once the dye powder has been mixed with water to make a dye solution, it will last three to four days if it is not activated by adding alkali. If refrigerated, it will last two to three weeks as the cold slows the dye's reaction with the water. Once the alkali activator has been added to the dye solution, either in the form of an activator mixture (part soda ash, part baking soda, see page 25) or as pure baking soda, the dye is good for only four hours.

Because you want to be sure you get a full four hours of use, never add pure soda ash, which is a strong alkali, to activate your dye solutions. If you do, 10 percent of the dye will react with the water in your cup in approximately 10 minutes, with another 10 percent the next 10 minutes. In a short

The background of these Thai Silks satin scarves were dyed with liquid fiber-reactive dyes. Then the dyes were thickened and sponged through the stencil openings to create the bamboo trellis, mixed flower borders, and wisteria designs (© Stencil Magic by Delta).

time, you could lose the dye's potency before it ever contacts the fabric. If you need more than four hours to complete a very complex process, you may want to consider the H series, which won't exhaust as quickly.

Procion® H Series

The H series dyes were developed specifically for direct application methods that were slower to execute, such as printing, stenciling, hand painting, and silkscreening. Because they have a slower reaction time than the MX series, they remain more stable once mixed with water. Accordingly, they are sold not only in powder form, but also as

Detail of COSMIC COWS by Carolyn A. Dahl. Fabric paint on dyed silk.

a liquid for those who wish to avoid working with the powders. The H powders keep as long as the MX powders, and the liquid H dyes will keep one year without color loss if the bottle is tightly capped and stored in a cool, dark place. Once diluted with chemical water to make the dye solutions, the H series will maintain color strength up to one month. Even after the alkali has been added, it will remain strong for one month as compared to the four hours for the MX series. The ability to keep a color usable for weeks makes them the perfect dyes for commissions, or for large printing projects where only a few yards can be completed in one day.

The H series has several other differences also. You will need to mix more colors yourself as fewer ready-made colors (17) are available. The H series is less convenient to use for immersion dyeing than the MX series as it requires a higher dyeing temperature (175 degrees Fahrenheit). Additionally, the H series dyes cannot be batch set (see page 28), but require heat for fixation—iron, clothes dryer, or steamer—with steam giving the most brilliant colors. And should you find yourself with left-over dye from both the MX and H series, resist mixing them together as they react at different rates and temperatures. However, the powdered H and the liquid H dyes can be combined.

Safety Precautions for Working with Fiber-Reactive Dyes

According to the manufacturer, fiber-reactive dyes are relatively non-toxic and pose no known health risks except for allergic reactions in sensitive individuals. However, do not use dyes when pregnant as no tests have included pregnant women so the health risks are unknown. Think about the technique that you're about to do and then use common sense. Your safety requirements can be quite different depending on the technique. Painting with thickened dyes may require only lightweight flexible surgical gloves once you've mixed the dyes. Whereas, sprayed dyes become airborne, and you'll not only want to wear a respirator and goggles but also long sleeves and pants to keep the dye off your body. If you want to know more about your dyes, you can request a MSDS (Material Safety Data Sheet) from your supplier. But in general, always follow these safety precautions:

- Purchase separate utensils for dyeing (plastic pans, measuring spoons, and cups)
- Confine your dyeing to your studio, garage, spare room, basement, or out-of-doors. If you must work in your kitchen, clear and cover your counters and be meticulous about cleanup afterwards.
- Do not eat, drink, or smoke while dyeing.
- Keep dyes, chemicals, and hot wax away from children and pets.
- Wear a dust mask or NIOSH-approved respirator with replaceable filters when mixing powdered dyes to avoid inhaling dye powders. If you wear contacts, wear safety goggles so no powder attaches to the lenses.
- Turn off fans and air conditioners when measuring out dye powders. Replace lids on containers and wipe up spilled powders or solutions immediately.
- Avoid skin contact with the dyes or auxiliary chemicals.

Fiber-reactive dyes can be used like watercolors, liquid and flowing (silk painting, spray-dyeing), or thickened to a paste for painting or printing. Either way, using them is like baking a cake, you follow the steps in recipes.

First I'll give the recipes (photocopy the page and pin it to your work room wall for easy reference) and the dyeing sequence. Then I'll answer the most frequently asked questions about each step and elaborate on the process or the ingredient's role. Don't skip the questions as they contain important information that you need to understand before using the dyes the first time. After you understand the function of the recipes' ingredients, you'll be able to solve your own dyeing problems and experiment with the book's techniques without adversely affecting the dyeing chemistry.

1. **Prepare the Chemical Water**

   In 2 cups of hot tap water dissolve 10 tablespoons of Urea. Add 2 cups cold water to make 1 quart of chemical water. If you have hard water, add 1 teaspoon of sodium hexametaphosphate (or Calgon, Metaphos, water softener) to the chemical water. Be sure the chemical water is cool before adding the dye.

2. **Add Dye to Chemical Water**

   Add 2 teaspoons powdered MX or H series fiber-reactive dye to 1 cup chemical water for a medium shade. Liquid H: follow manufacturer's instructions.

3. **Activate the Dye Solution**

   (*Use Method 1 or 2*)

   Method 1: Alkali Activator Added to Fabric

   Dissolve 9 tablespoons of soda ash in 1 gallon of warm water (95 degrees Fahrenheit). Soak fabric for 15 minutes. Wring out excess solution but do not rinse.

Method 2: Alkali Activator Added to Dye In Container

For cotton and rayon: Add 1 teaspoon activator mixture to 1 cup dye solution. The activator mixture is made by combining two alkalis: 4 parts baking soda and 1 part soda ash (or Pro Chem Activator). For example, place 4 teaspoons baking soda in a jar and add 1 teaspoon soda ash and stir well. Take 1 teaspoon of this "mixture" and add it to the cup of dye solution. *For silk:* Add 1 teaspoon baking soda (a milder alkali) to 1 cup of dye solution.

4. **Thicken Dyes if Desired**

   To make 1 cup of paste: Add $5^{1}/_{2}$ tablespoons of ProPaste Mix SH to 1 cup room temperature tap water, adding and mixing a little at a time. Let the mixture set for 4 to 6 hours or overnight. When the thickened paste is ready, the dye can be added directly to the paste. Dissolve the powdered dye first in a little chemical water. Add approximately 2 teaspoons powdered dye to 1 cup of paste. If adding liquid dye, the amount can be judged visually.

   When you are ready to activate the dye paste, dissolve 1 teaspoon activator mixture in a small amount of chemical water and add to one cup of dye paste. For silk, use 1 teaspoon baking soda per cup. To thin the dye paste, use chemical water mixed from 7 teaspoons urea per 1 cup tap water.

5. **Complete your chosen technique.**

6. **Heat Set Finished Fabric and Rinse** (in water with or without Synthrapol®).

   Batching: Cover fabric in plastic for 24 to 48 hours. (For MX dyes only.)

   Ironing: Iron each section of the fabric about 3 to 5 minutes at medium heat.

   Clothes Dryer: Tumble for 45 to 60 minutes (not for silk).

   Steaming: Consult instructions on page 28.

Get to know the personalities of your dyes by dyeing small draw string silk pouches from Thai Silks.

1. Why do I need to use chemical water?

In immersion dyeing, the fabric is submerged in a container filled with a one-color dye bath. As the fabric stays in the dye bath for anywhere from 20 to 60 minutes, the chemical action of the dye has plenty of time to react with the wet fiber. In direct application methods, however, the dyeing takes place on the surface of the fabric. The dye dries quickly, shortening the time the dye can bond with the wet fiber. So to ensure that the proper dyeing conditions occur during direct application methods, several auxiliary chemicals are added to the water in which the dyes are mixed, hence the name chemical water.

Urea pellets are made from an ammonia compound containing 46 percent nitrogen and help to maintain moisture in the fabric so the dyes have longer to complete their reactions. They also aid in dissolving the dye particles when mixing dyes with the water. If you work in a very humid environment, the amount of urea can be reduced slightly. But never go below six tablespoons of urea per quart of water. Urea can be purchased from dye suppliers or a fertilizer store (ask for "tapioca" urea). Sodium hexametaphosphate (Calgon, water softener, Metaphos) is added to regular tap water to neutralize any minerals (metallic ions) that could interfere with the dye's action.

2. What is the easiest method for mixing powdered dyes?

Put on your face mask, goggles, and rubber gloves. Turn off fans and air conditioners. Pour one cup of chemical water into a measuring cup. Then pour a small amount from the measuring cup into a plastic or glass container. Remove lid from the powdered dye, spoon out two teaspoons (to achieve a medium shade), replace lid, and place powder on top of chemical water in the container. Stir until a smooth paste is formed. Add remaining water from the measuring cup into the container. You now have one cup of dye solution in a stock color (as it comes from the manufacturer).

If any powder has spilled on a surface, wipe it up with a wet paper towel. Once the powdered dye

has dissolved and can no longer be inhaled, your mask and goggles can be removed. If you are using liquid H dyes instead of the powdered dyes, follow the manufacturer's recommendations for dilution proportions.

3. How can I overcome my fear of mixing colors?

First of all, remember that fiber-reactive dyes are economical, so you can experiment freely with colors. It's just a little dye. And although you may not believe it at first, you already have a good sense of color, or you couldn't shop for clothes or decorate your home. You make color selections all the time in real life, so trust your choices.

To overcome a fear of mixing dyes, you simply need to get to know the colors. I suggest you paint 3" x 3" fabric squares in each color you like, in a light, medium, and dark value (all colors dry lighter). Or, instead of the squares, purchase a quantity of inexpensive items (silk handkerchiefs, small scarves, drawstring bags—available from Thai Silks, see Supply Sources) and dye each a different color. You'll learn quickly that each color has a distinct personality and loves to surprise the dyer.

Unlike pigments, which are inert and predictable in mixtures, dyes can be quirky and lively. For instance, if I mix the MX turquoise and fushia together I will get the wonderful purple I'm expecting. However, when I brush the color onto the fabric, the turquoise often separates and rushes ahead of the mixture. If allowed to dry on its own, I will have a beautiful purple shape edged in turquoise where I expected a solid purple color. I've also learned that turquoise may give the appearance of being aggressive, but it washes out more than other colors during rinsing; I always mix it stronger. Fushia on the other hand may be slow moving, but it penetrates and stains the fabric quickly and permanently. So a little powder goes a long way. And if I want a true black area on silk, I don't use fiber-reactive dyes at all, but switch to a silk dye.

Studying color reference books is always helpful in understanding how color works,[6] but stop reading immediately if color paralysis sets in.

Remember that color is not only scientific, but a joyous emotional component of our lives. Have fun with it.

4. Should I add activator to the dye solution or presoak my fabric?

It's really a personal preference based on how you work. Both the MX and H series require an alkali activator to start the chemical reaction between the fiber and dye molecules. Think of the alkali as a catalyst that gets the molecules moving about and forming the chemical links (if you forget the alkali your color will wash out during rinsing). The alkalis commonly used are soda ash (also known as sodium carbonate, washing soda, sal soda, and "fixer"), baking soda (bicarbonate of soda), or an activator mixture (a combination of the two). Do not purchase the washing soda sold in supermarkets as it has additives that will interfere with the dyeing process. Also replace your baking soda frequently as it needs to be fresh.

Fiber-reactive dyes may be activated with alkali in two ways. In Method 1, the fabric is soaked beforehand in soda ash so the activator is already in the fabric when the dye is applied. The advantages of this method are: large amounts of fabric can be prepared easily in the machine (don't rinse), the fabric can be painted wet or stored for future use, you don't have to remember to add activator to the container of dye each time, the MX dye solutions last longer than four hours because they aren't activated, and the soda ash solution can be reused until it weakens.

Method 2, where the activator is added to liquid dye in the container, is preferred by some people because the soda ash (in Method 1) in the soaked fabric irritates their skin. Method 2 is also the best method for silk as the time the alkali (even the milder baking soda) contacts the silk is reduced. For busy people who want to finish a small project in four hours, it eliminates any beforehand preparing of the fabric.

5. How can I thicken dye so it's more like paint?

For some techniques, the dye will need to be thickened to slow its movement through the fabric or to control bleeding in painting or printing methods.

The most common ingredient used to thicken dye is sodium alginate, which comes from a species of seaweed. It can be purchased separately, often called thickener, or simply alginate, or by various brand names. Or, it can be purchased in combination with other ingredients as a print paste mix, so named because it is most often used with printing processes. Either way, the dried sodium alginate powder (which will keep approximately two years) swells when added to water making a gelatinous substance into which the dye can be suspended.

Unlike starches or gums, sodium alginate thickeners do not chemically bond with the fabric's structure nor react with the fiber-reactive dye. Thus the maximum conditions for dyeing are maintained because it doesn't interfere. The thickener is easily removed during the rinsing procedure.

Two types of sodium alginate are available. The first is known as a high viscosity, low solids type of alginate (such as Pro Thick SH), which will yield a very thick paste with a small amount of alginate powder. It can be used on all fabrics and is the one I've used for the techniques in this book, but other brands can be substituted. If, however, you need a very fine line definition on a lightweight fabric such as China silk, then a second type (low viscosity, high solids) can be used (such as Pro Thick F). Follow the manufacturer's instructions for this second type as more will be needed to achieve the same paste thickness.

The thickener can be mixed to any degree of viscosity. I generally prefer to make a very thick paste and thin it as needed for different techniques. The paste will keep for several months in the refrigerator if no dye activator has been added. Mark the jars "do not drink" and seal the lids with tape as an extra precaution. If you prefer to use another thickener other than the ProPaste Mix listed in the recipe section, follow the manufacturer's instructions.

6. Do I really have to steam-set my fabrics? I can't afford a professional steamer.

You don't have to steam-set fabrics if you use MX

Fiber-reactive dyes can be thickened and used like paint to create designs that don't bleed on the fabric.

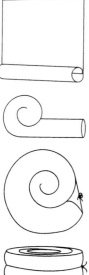

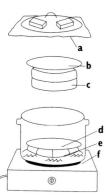

To prepare the fabric for steaming, roll it in blank newsprint, coil the tube into a spiral, and secure it with string.

dyes; there are other options. The H series does have to be steamed, but simple, inexpensive steamers can be made from canning pots. All fabrics, however, do have to be set with one of the following easy methods in order for the dyes to be permanent and colorfast.

Batch Setting (or Batching) | Before the fabric dries, cover completely in a sheet of plastic and allow to dry as slowly as possible. If the fabric is damp, it can be sandwiched between two plastic sheets and rolled up to save space. If the fabric is very wet, however, it must be covered and left in place to dry. The fabric should remain moist for a minimum of four hours if you are rushed, but 24 to 48 is better. The room temperature must be 70 degrees or above during that time period. If your studio temperature drops too low at night, or if the fabric dries too quickly, the dyes will not set properly. Remember that batch setting is for MX dyes only. The H series requires heat setting.

Iron Setting | Slowly move a medium hot iron over a small section of the fabric for about 3 to 5 minutes. Iron temperatures vary, so although you want the hottest temperature appropriate to your fabric, beware of scorching (cover fabrics painted with thickened dye with scrap fabric to protect iron). Try to keep all the fabric in that one area warm for the full amount of time. When one section is set, move to the next. Although this is a rather tedious activity, it doesn't require much concentration and can be done while enjoying your favorite television programs.

Clothes Dryer Setting | Fabrics, except silk, that are completely dry may also be set by tumbling for 45 to 60 minutes in a clothes dryer set at the hottest setting. Commercial dryers are best as they reach higher temperatures. Avoid putting fabrics with resists (gutta, wax) into the dryer as some of the materials could melt and stick to the machine.

Steam Setting | Steam setting is the only method where you can be sure that your fabric is reaching the proper temperature and moisture to set the dyes in a controlled environment. The effectiveness of other methods can vary depending on your equipment, your mood, the ambient moisture, room temperature, etc. Best of all, steaming yields the brightest colors with the least washout and allows you to set many yards of fabric

in an hour. If you work with wax processes, it can not only set the dyes but remove most of the wax at the same time.

Canning Pot Steamer | Although professional steamers are available, a very efficient and economical home steamer can be made from a large enamel canning pot with a wire bottle rack, which will hold the fabric above the water.

Before placing the fabric in the steamer, it must be protected from condensation. The easiest method is to sandwich the fabric between sheets of blank newsprint (available as packing paper from moving companies) rolled into a tube and coiled into a loose spiral-shaped bundle. The newsprint protects the fabric from water spots and also absorbs melting wax. The bundle is secured with string or wrapped with masking tape and must be small enough to fit into the pot without touching the sides or the lid.

Place the canning pot on the stove or an electric hot plate. Fill the pot with 1" to 2" of water; the depth depends on the elevation of the bottle rack. Place a layer of old newspapers cut in a circle on the rack to keep splashes from below from reaching the bottom of the fabric. Do not allow the newspapers to touch the sides of the pot. Turn on the heat, cover, and when steam rises, set the fabric bundle on the newspaper-covered rack. Place another layer of newspapers on top to catch any condensation from the lid.

Next, lay a folded towel or more newspaper over the opening of your pot. Let it extend over the edge of the pot to prevent steam from escaping. Weight the cover with a few bricks to help build pressure. Be sure the towel or newspaper does not extend too far over the edge of the pot or it may catch fire.

Begin timing. How long to steam will depend on the type of dye, fabric density, and the amount. MX dyes will fix in a shorter time (approximately 20 minutes) than the H series (approximately 45 minutes). A thinner fabric such as China silk will allow the steam to penetrate more quickly than a dense cotton fabric. And, of course, if you have a half yard in the steamer versus three yards, it's obvious that the steaming times will differ. With experimentation, you will arrive at the right temperature and time for your equipment.

The canning pot steamer
a. towel or newspaper
b. old newspapers cut in circle
c. fabric bundle
d. old newspapers
e. rack
f. heat source

Remove the lid carefully to allow the steam to escape before reaching inside. Remove the fabric bundle and unroll partially. If it has steamed sufficiently, tiny wrinkles, or puckers, will appear at various points throughout the fabric's surface. If not, roll again and steam a bit longer. After steaming, wait at least 24 hours before rinsing.

Vertical Steamer | If very wide fabric or many yards need to be steamed, the canning pot can easily be extended into a vertical steamer. Place a 10" wide, 5- to 6-foot long stove pipe or galvanized steel air conditioner duct pipe into the canning pot. Roll the fabric (sandwiched between paper) onto a cardboard fabric tube or chicken wire formed into a tube and secure with tape. Lower the tube into the pipe and suspend it from some type of hanging device (bent hanger, dowel rod) so it doesn't touch the water in the bottom of the canning pot. Cover top of pipe with newspaper, put on the lid and steam. Be sure pipe is balanced and secured in the canning pot so it won't wobble or fall over when boiling begins. The pipe gets very hot during steaming, so do not allow children or pets to go near.

> To me, pulling fabric from steam clouds is the perfect finale to the creative process. Like a potter who gives the clay piece to the kiln to be transformed, I like the idea of giving my finished fabric to the heat of a steaming pot. Even if the colors didn't become more brilliant, I would probably steam anyhow as the ritual attracts me. I enjoy listening for the pot to sing, throwing in my lucky penny, watching steam rise on a cold day, smelling the hot fabric as it unrolls. But for you, the pleasure might be in the slow movement of a heavy iron sliding across color, or the tumbling sound of a dryer as you rush about doing other things, or the sight of glistening fabric marinating under plastic. Try all four setting options. Find the method that fits your space, lifestyle, and natural working rhythms. A process is only hard if it gives no pleasure.

7. When I rinse my fabric, color comes out. Did I do something wrong?

No. When the fiber molecules make a complete bond with the dye molecules, they are full, so to speak, and don't absorb more dye. So all fabrics dyed with fiber-reactive dyes will have some unused dye and chemicals lingering in the fibers that needs to be rinsed away. The fabric will look slightly lighter after rinsing, but then will hold its color well in subsequent washings.

If you don't need the fabric immediately, it's preferable to allow the dye to age a minimum of 24 hours or up to a week before rinsing. Sort the pieces into color groups. To hand rinse, begin with cool water and keep the fabric moving. Remember to wear rubber gloves. Continue rinsing until water runs clear; then do a final wash with soap and warm water. If using a machine, fill it to the highest level with cool water, no soap, and add the fabric after agitation has begun. Wash on a short cycle, three to five minutes, then switch the dial to spin to drain off most of the colored water. Don't allow it to complete the spin cycle. Immediately reset the dial to a warm wash. After rinsing and spinning, stop the machine, open out the fabric, and remove any knots. If the fabric feels slimy, some of the alkali activator is still present. Reset machine for a hot water wash with a mild detergent and let it complete this cycle. For silk, use a mild dish washing detergent such as Ivory, Palmolive, or Joy.

If you have a lot of white or light-colored areas in your designs, you may want to use a special detergent called Synthrapol® (2 teaspoons per gallon hot water or 3 tablespoons to $^1/_4$ cup per washer load—don't use on silk). Besides its use as a scouring agent in preparing fabric, Synthrapol® also removes the unreacted dye from the fabric and suspends it so it doesn't deposit onto another area. Should you discover that a color has migrated into unwanted areas, wash the fabric again immediately. The longer the escaping color stays in the fabric, the more permanent the stain becomes.

Disposal of Dyes

Do not pour your dyes onto the ground. They can reach underground water levels or wash into streams. Most dyes and auxiliary chemicals in the amounts studio dyers use can be disposed of in city sewer systems where they will undergo treatment. Flush the spent dye down the drain with lots of additional water to dilute the mixture. If you have a septic system, contact your local water department for guidelines.

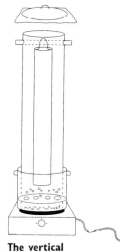

The vertical steamer

FABRIC PAINTS

right:
SPACE AGE ETHNIC By Carolyn A. Dahl and Lisa Sharp. When my collaborator and I were chosen to participate in The Diamond Collection fashion show, I wanted to try something different. Because one of the sponsors was a batting company, Fairfield Processing Corporation, I decided to try to paint batting as if it were cloth. Instead of sandwiching it between two pieces of fabric, however, I wanted to use it as the outer fabric. When the Cotton Classic batting absorbed the Createx fabric paint, I was happy to discover that it became very felt-like, almost like handmade paper. Once it was quilted onto a background fabric, it was durable enough to survive a year of traveling to fashion shows around the country. Photo: courtesy of Fairfield Processing Corporation. Photographer: Brad Stanton.

Painted batting can be used for small purses, hats, and numerous other craft projects. Photo by Aileen Guggenheim.

right:
Detail of painted quilt batting. Photo by Mike McCormick.

The fabric paints that we use are similar to fine artist's acrylic paints, which appeared in their water-based form around 1956. They consist of a pigment (the coloring agent) suspended in a polymer resin, which acts as the binder or glue. Acrylic resins are the most common, found in artist's acrylic paints, but other formulations are also used. Each resin gives the fabric a particular feel, which may be stiff, rubbery, or soft. After application of the paint, the water evaporates, leaving a strong film of color that is flexible, has good resistance to fading, and is insoluble once dry.

Several characteristics make using fabric paints different from using dyes. Dyes are transparent, joining their color with the color of the ground fabric to make a new color. With paints, however, you have several choices: transparent, semi-transparent, or opaque (when you want to completely cover the background color with a new color). Not only is a large range of colors available in these three types, but also in many specialty paints that achieve unusual effects: metallic, pearlescent, interference (reflects its complementary color), glitter, fluorescent, paint-on fibers and stars, and even glow in the dark. The paints may also be used

SHAMAN'S COAT by Margaret Scott-Dobbins. Createx metallic and pearlescent paint on leather, embellished with feathers, turquoise, bones.

as colored glue for attaching jewels or embellishments to the fabric.

Fabric paints are extremely easy to use. No special equipment, set up, health precautions (other than don't ingest the colors), or additional chemicals are required. You don't need to memorize recipes as the paints come ready-to-use and require no technical information to assure chemical reactions. The only heat setting required is ironing to increase wash fastness and even that step has been eliminated by many manufacturers. The completed fabric doesn't even need to be rinsed, unless a newly painted odor remains.

Another advantage (unlike dyes which are fiber specific) is that paints will work on almost any fiber or blend as long as it is free of surface treatments—even cotton quilt batting (try Fairfield's Cotton Classic and Hobbs Heirloom battings). It's great to be able to grab an old fabric whose content you've long ago forgotten and start painting without any worry.

Every technique from fine lines and precise edges to wet watercolor washes to printing techniques can be created with the same jar of paint. If you like working in very wet washes, however, beware of diluting the paint too much and reducing its adhesive properties. It is best to purchase the manufacturer's extender which will allow you to dilute the color without breaking down the binder as plain water would. Also remember that if you like to work in the opposite way with thicker applications, the paint's binder will tend to stiffen the fabric slightly and have a plastic feel if used too heavily. However, slightly stiffened fabric is the perfect ground for designs you want to embellish with free-motion machine stitching.

Although fabric paints have good fade resistance to ultraviolet light because the pigments are not chemically reactive like dyes, the colors are not as resistant to abrasion. After repeated machine washings, the agitation may break down the paint's binder that holds the color to the surface, and little by little the pigment rinses away lessening the vitality of the color. Of course, this is no problem if you're doing a wall piece that is seldom laundered. But if you use fabric paints on wearables, always turn the garment inside out and wash by hand or on a very gentle cycle to prevent this color loss.

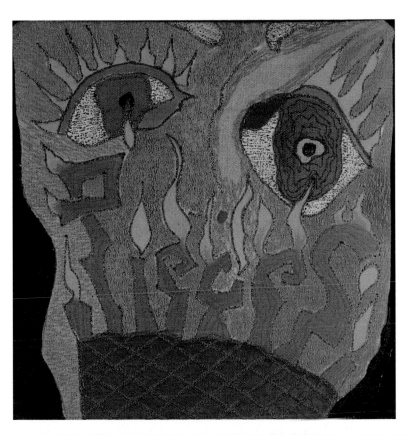

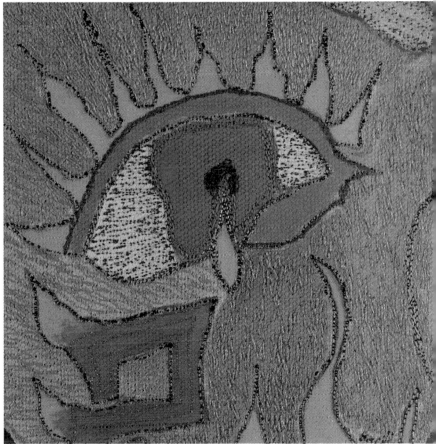

BIRTHDAY BREAKDOWN by Carolyn A. Dahl. Fabric paint on cotton and free motion stitching.

When purchasing fabric paints, it is best to use those offered by textile dye suppliers or to stick with name brands. You want a quality paint that has a high concentration of light-resistant pigments and a pure binder with no added impurities to affect permanent adhesion. If a particular name brand is listed in the technique instructions, it means that I have obtained the best results with that product. It does not mean that others won't work. Any water-based fabric paint may be substituted, but the final effect could be slightly different.

Fabric paint may be called different names depending on the supplier: textile pigments, textile paints, fabric colors, fabric inks, and airbrush inks (thin, filtered, concentrated pigment). The products may all be pigments suspended in a synthetic binder, but vary in concentration, quality, viscosity, and additives. It is a good idea not to intermix brands as the chemical formulations may vary. Be sure, however, that the products you select are designated for fabric or the binder will not give a soft hand to your fabric.

You can also purchase concentrated pigments separately (Liquid Pure Pigment Colors from Createx) and add them to the proper binder (also called medium) to make your own fabric paints. For instance, if one day you're stamping on black fabric, you add your pigment to the opaque medium so the paint will cover the dark background. However, the next day you may want a transparent, sprayed color, so you add the same pigment to a thin airbrush medium, etc. This method reduces the different types of fabric paint you need to purchase and store. It also allows you to control the concentration of pigment particles on your fabric. Interesting granulation effects can be achieved by variations in the pigment-to-binder ratio. (Add a fair amount of liquid pigment to diluted binder and pour or paint it on manipulated fabric (silk works best). Allow the fabric to dry undisturbed. The pigment will settle and collect in areas as it dries, creating a granular effect.)

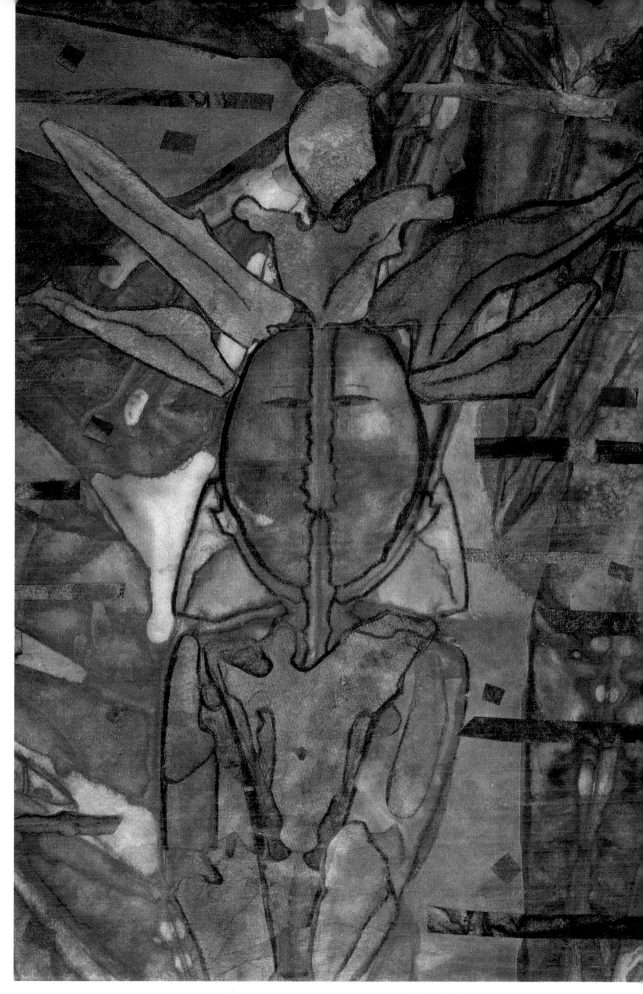

NATURE SPIRIT by Carolyn A. Dahl. Thickened dyes, fabric paint, granulation, collage of silk. Photo by Maria Davila.

CHAPTER THREE

Black-and-White Transformations

MY WHITE CAT DOESN'T KNOW what a dangerous life he leads. As he passes through my studio, brushing against dye pots, I watch his smooth white surface. Lucky for him, he never stands still for long nor sleeps too soundly near me. So far, he's a normal colored cat, but I keep dreaming about his other eight lives. Surely one of them could have pink tipped whiskers.

Moonstone is not the only animal whose surface I've wanted to color. My idea for this process came from zebras. Watching their shifting black-and-white patterns at the zoo one day, I mentally began to color in the white stripes. I suddenly realized they had given me a good idea for transforming commercial fabric. I went right from the zoo to a nearby fabric store and purchased a yard of every black-and-white print they had. I even found a zebra stripe design in cotton flannelette. The soft nap had an uncanny resemblance to zebra skin.

Once home, I splashed, poured, sprayed, and painted dye on the fabrics. After drying, the black-and-white print had become multicolored. The black parts of the pattern were still black, but the once-white areas glowed with bright colors.

Fabric companies inspire us with an endless array of black-and-white prints. All the beginner has to do is pour, dip, paint, spray on color for beautiful, usable fabrics for any sewing project.

FIVE GOOD BEGINNER'S TECHNIQUES

Whether I had applied the colors carefully or haphazardly, all the fabrics were usable. The black patterns held the design together no matter what I did in the white areas. So if you've never painted fabric in your life, transforming black-and-white prints is an excellent starting technique. You'll learn various application methods, get to know your dyes and paints, and gain confidence with color. Best of all, you simply cannot fail because the black will hide mistakes, so you'll never waste fabric.

Although black-and-white prints give the best and most dramatic results, other combinations can also be used (red and white, blue and white). The only difference is that black absorbs other colors without changing its own color; whereas a red or blue will combine with the applied color to form a new one. For instance, if you are painting blue into the white area of a red-and-white fabric, the blue could bleed beyond the white and into the red, creating a purple or darkened edge around the shape. Not that this would be bad. Some very wonderful, unusual, and surprising shades can result depending on how deeply the hand-painted color is able to penetrate the commercially printed color.

When purchasing fabrics to transform, look for prints in which the white areas dominate. The more white space the fabric has, the more area for you to color. Prepare your fabric as usual, and use either dyes (thin or slightly thickened) or diluted fabric paints, depending on the fiber content of your fabric. Remember you can't fail. The learning will take place while you do the process, so begin with these techniques and then invent your own.

ZEBRA JACKET by Carolyn Dahl. Hand-dyed cotton flannelette. Dedicated to the zoo zebras who inspired the technique.

When the unpainted black-and-white fabric is placed next to the transformed fabric, you can see how the hand painting softens and personalizes the commercially printed pattern.

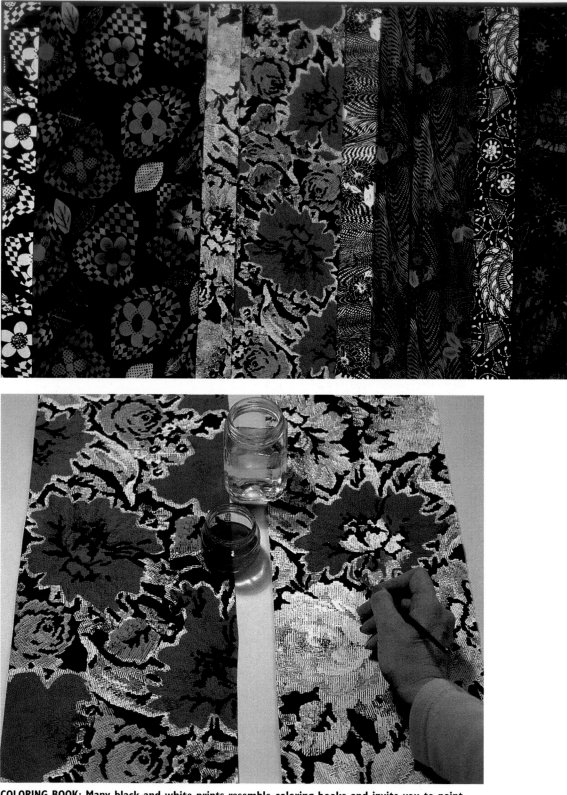

COLORING BOOK: Many black-and-white prints resemble coloring books and invite you to paint them with their large scale designs, flowers, animals, or geometric forms. To prevent color from bleeding into an adjacent shape, use thickened dyes. Or, if you prefer non-thickened colors, tape the dry fabric to paper which will absorb some dye, don't overload your brush with color, and stop painting before you reach the shape's edge. If the dye still spreads too quickly, blot the shape with a paper towel.

SELECTIVE FOCUS: Sometimes an intriguing shape, hidden in the overall black-and-white pattern, can be emphasized through color. Adding the light blue and green dye to the leopard's face in this heavily-patterned print, makes it mysteriously emerge from the darker background.

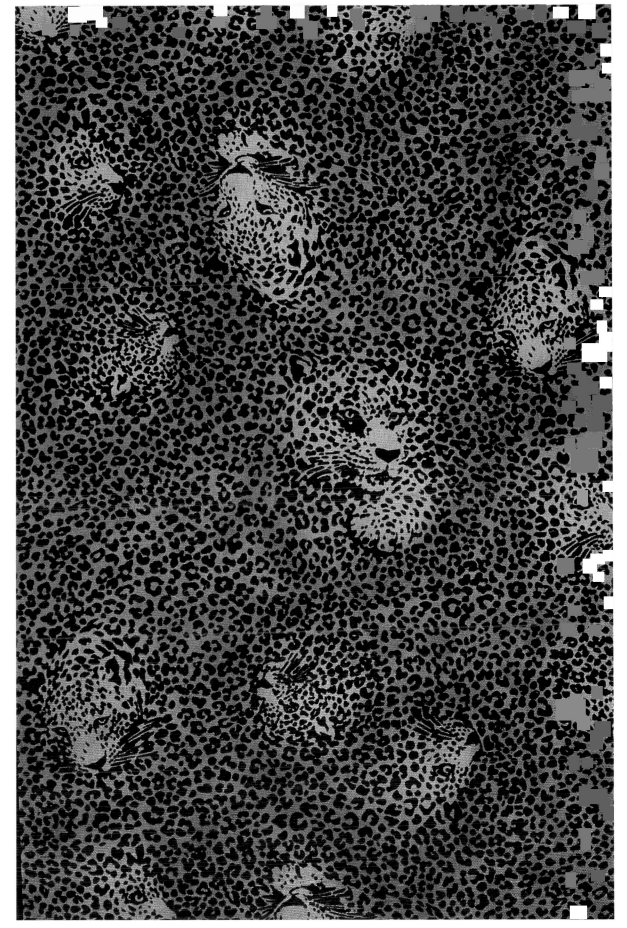

SPRAYED PATTERNS: Start with a polka dot print. Lay a large net, plastic grid, or openwork fabric (to act as a mask) over the print. Spray the surface with dye. When the mask is removed, there'll be a pattern behind the polka dots, giving a sense of depth to the fabric. (See also page 99.) The center panel with its cats and flowers is a good example of a color book pattern.

LINEAR BLEED: Select fabrics with energetic black lines on an open white background. Put yourself into a spontaneous mood. Load your brush with color and trace the curve of a spiral, zip down a zigzagged line, circle a dot, or spatter a shape. Allow the colors to spread, but leave a lot of white background to provide contrast. If you need inspiration, study pictures of Oriental calligraphy or Joan Miró's paintings. Be childlike and have fun with this process. (Notice how the blue dye created a shadow in the red-and-white background fabric.)

COLOR BANDS AND BLOTCHES: Painting bands of color across your fabric creates a sense of movement, as if a stream of water were flowing behind the black-and-white pattern. If the print has large open areas of white, the bands will be more visible and the directional pull stronger. Try a variety of lines: vertical, horizontal, diagonal, curved, broken, thin, or thick. Instead of bands, random blotches of color can be scattered across wet fabric (dip or spray fabric first). The different colors will bleed together to create blended backgrounds.

CHAPTER FOUR

Water Drop Patterns

"Wherever you go today, tomorrow, or the rest of your life,
you are part of someone's visual landscape.
Why not make it beautiful?"

[C. DAHL, WEARABLE ART LECTURE]

WHENEVER I SPEND TOO MUCH time indoors, I begin to miss the sky. Sitting under artificial lights all day makes me realize how fortunate I am to be an artist. To have the freedom to step outside any time of the day, watch birds soar, feel the breeze as I work, or stand in the rain are reasons enough to have spent my life in the arts.

BLUE NORTHER COAT by Carolyn A. Dahl and Lisa Sharp. The sprayed fabric has been embellished with stitchery, applique, beading, hand-dyed lace, and cord for a more luxurious coat. Photograph by Mike McCormick.

RAIN CLOTH

Because hand-painted fabric, especially silk, that hasn't been set is susceptible to water spotting, I often take advantage of the rain's patterning ability. When a sprinkle arrives, I grab newly painted fabric, which I've attached to cardboard beforehand, and rush outside. If there is no lightning, I enjoy standing by the fabric watching the drops move the dye around. Persuading the rain to stop at just the right point in my fabric design, however, has never been easy. So sometimes I have to make my own rain.

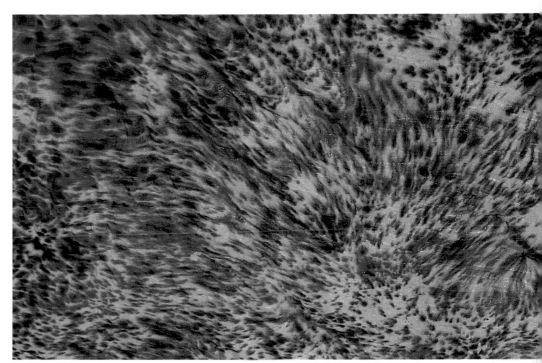

Procedure

When I saw Cheri Ruzich's hand-painted cloth, it reminded me of my silk rain cloth patterns. On a sunny day, she places the cloth over grass, squirts on fabric inks, and uses her garden hose to create the effects of rain. The images of her sky-filled studio and a landscape covered in colored cloth were so appealing, I asked Cheri to share her technique for making water-dappled cotton fabric.

Water drop fabric by Cheri Ruzich. Photo by Margaret Mitchell.

Cheri Ruzich's outdoor studio filled with colored cloth drying in the sun. Photo by Margaret Mitchell.

Air brush ink is squirted onto the moist fabric and misted with a garden hose to blend the colors.

5 Squirt the inks onto the fabric. The position of the squirt bottle will influence how the ink falls and the pattern. With the bottle spout straight up, little droplets will result. If you point the spout toward the fabric, the ink comes out in a steady stream that makes good lines. Holding the bottle horizontally will give large droplets and allow more control over your pattern placement.

6 Adjust the nozzle of the hose until a fine, even spray is produced, then pivot toward the fabric and mist it one or two times. Do not over saturate the cloth.

7 Allow the fabric to dry undisturbed in direct sunlight. If you don't like the pattern, wash it immediately and most of the color will be removed.

8 Heat set the dry fabric with an iron set at the highest temperature your fabric can bear (20 to 30 seconds in well-ventilated room) or use a commercial dryer (25 minutes). Most home dryers will not reach the 250 degree temperature necessary to set the inks. After heat setting, machine wash the cloth on a gentle, short cycle with regular laundry detergent to soften the fabric.

1 Pick a sunny spot in your yard on a day when no rain is predicted and begin work in the morning or early afternoon to ensure sufficient drying time.

2 Wash 5 to 10 yards of fabric cut into desired lengths. Place wet fabric in a plastic bag.

3 Dilute the air brush inks using 3 parts ink to 7 parts water. Pour the diluted inks into squirt bottles and shake to mix well.

4 Remove one length of washed fabric from the plastic bag, spread it on the yard, and secure its four corners. (Cheri recommends 9-gauge fence ties, which are thin wire rods for attaching cyclone fence material to the poles. She pushes the ties into the ground, one at each corner of the fabric, and attaches the cloth with clothespins.)

Water drop fabric by Cheri Ruzich.

Supplies

- Versatex Air Brush Ink (assorted colors)
- Fabric: White, 100% cotton print cloth (#400 from Testfabrics) or any other natural or synthetic fabric without surface treatments.
- Squirt bottles (narrow spouts, with caps)
- Fabric anchors (bricks, stakes, 9-gauge fence ties)
- Garden hose with fine spray nozzle (with handle)
- Plastic drop cloth (if working on driveway or patio)

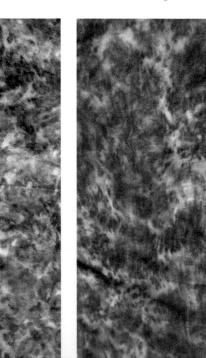

SPRAY CLOTH

Air surrounds us everyday. We cut through it as we walk and pull it in and out of our bodies every second. Yet it's only when we suddenly catch its dancing dust in a beam of sunlight do we believe it exists. By painting with a sprayer, however, we can reveal its invisible presence whenever we want. When dye or paint is propelled through a nozzle, it mingles with the air, dropping onto the fabric as tiny dots, much like fallen air bubbles. The artist never touches the fabric with hand nor brush. This colored bubble texture is what gives sprayed fabric its distinctive beauty. One always feels the dyed air in the process.

Simply spraying many different colors and letting them blend optically on a flat fabric can yield beautiful, misty, atmospheric effects. Or the fabric can be manipulated into folds, pleats, or other dimensional forms. When sprayed, only the top surface receives the color, causing free form abstract shapes when the fabric is unfolded.

If you want more control over the color development and shape placement, stencils can be used to develop more definite patterns. A stencil can be anything that blocks the dye or paint from reaching the fabric while preserving the color underneath. Even prehistoric dwellers knew the simple principle of a stencil. In the cave paintings of Lascaux (France), some early artist placed a hand on the wall and sprayed color around it. Generations later, we still ponder this simple hand shape and wonder what tool served as a primitive sprayer, perhaps a hollow bone or cane.[1]

Stencils can be as simple as your hand, or as complex as an intricate Japanese stencil cut from paper impregnated with persimmon juice and smoke. Many objects from our everyday lives work

Melody Johnson arranged her fabric into gentle folds before spraying, leaving lots of white for a snow covered mountain effect in her HOLLY-HOCKS quilt.

well as stencils also, such as stick-on labels, doilies, plastic templates, feathers, masking tape, gutter screen, leaves, etc. So experiment.

In the following procedure, torn newspapers are used as stencils with fiber-reactive dye as the colorant to produce abstract shapes. Fabric paint (diluted to spraying consistency) or airbrush inks may be substituted. Plant and hair spray pump bottles give irregular spray patterns and interest-ing drips. Preval® sprayers give a smooth spray. Found at auto or paint supply stores, they have a glass bottle on the bottom with a screw-on canis-ter of propellant (the power unit on top).[2] Remember to add dye activator to all spray bottles if using fiber-reactive dyes (dissolve activator first in a small amount of water to prevent granules from clogging the nozzle or presoak the fabric in soda ash, see page 25).

Preval® Sprayer: Fill the 6-ounce glass container with the dye, attach the power unit, and spray. The power unit can be purchased separately and the glass con-tainers reused.

Scrunching and folding the fabric before spraying produces free-form shapes as only the top surface of the fabric receives color.

below: Details of BLUE NORTHER COAT by Carolyn A. Dahl and Lisa Sharp.

The basic process is simple as newspaper stencils are placed on the fabric and a color sprayed into the uncovered fabric areas. The stencils are moved to a new position and another color sprayed on. The process is repeated and new paper shapes added until you're satisfied with the color overlays and pattern density.

As sprayed dye is easily inhaled, wear a protective mask or respirator. Avoid contact with the spray by wearing rubber gloves and long sleeves. Work outside on a calm day (you may need to weight fabric edges and newspaper stencils) or in a garage. Cover nearby objects as dye spray can drift.

1 Arrange torn or cut newspaper shapes (with a few pieces of double-stick tape on backside) on the fabric.

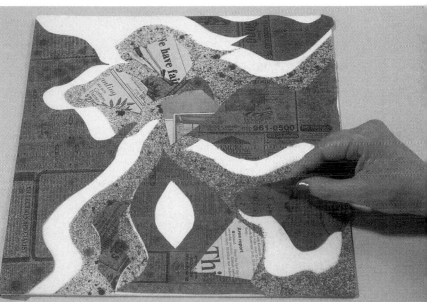

2 Lightly spray the first color (pink) over the open areas of fabric. Avoid spraying at an angle which may shoot spray under the stencil edge. You want distinct dots of color, not solid color, so don't over saturate the fabric.

3 Allow the fabric to absorb some of the first color before moving the stencils or the color will bleed into the shape. Re-position the newspaper stencils. Move some stencils to reveal a white edge of fabric, remove or add shapes, cut holes or alter shapes, and cover areas of the pink with new paper to save that color.

4 Lightly spray on the turquoise color. Wherever the turquoise dye lands on pink areas, the two will combine into purple. When the turquoise falls on a newly-exposed white area, that section will become turquoise. Pink areas covered by stencils will remain pink.

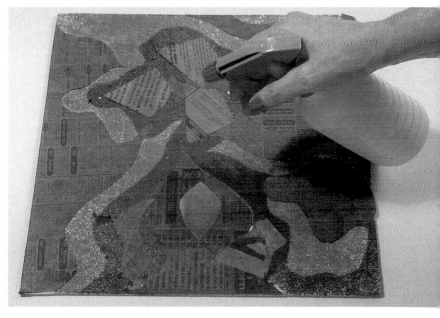

5 Continue this process. I can spray about five colors before the dots disappear and muddy areas develop. If the newspaper stencils become too wet at any time, replace them or they will not block the dye. Leave the last stencils in place until the fabric is fairly dry.

below:

6 A finished fabric where large areas of white have been left unsprayed.

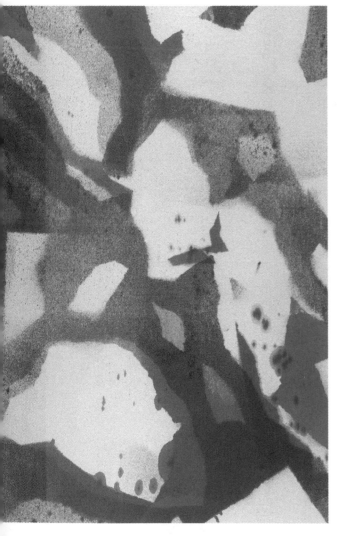

right:

I don't recommend batch setting as keeping the fabric moist could cause sharp edges to bleed and become less definite. However, painting over a freshly sprayed design with a new color or pure chemical water causes it to migrate into interesting patterns.

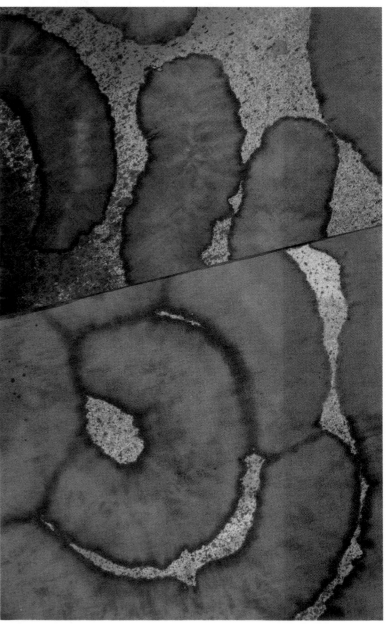

WATER DROP YARDAGE

The rain and spray patterns are perfect techniques for producing yardage for home decor projects (curtains, upholstery, pillows, bedspreads) because the investment in supplies is low, the process is completed quickly, and you don't even need an indoor workroom. For clothing artists, the soft droplet patterns are very wearable as is, or the fabric can be embellished further with stitching, quilting, or beading for a more luxurious garment.

The newspaper stencil technique creates a very wearable coat or jacket design without any further embellishment by Carolyn A. Dahl. Fiber-reactive dyes on cotton corduroy. See page 42 for embellished version.

CHAPTER FIVE

Nature's Patterns

PERHAPS NATURE HERSELF TAUGHT the first person to make nature prints. Robert Little in his book NATURE PRINTING¹ quotes Henry Bradbury: "Nature, in her mysterious operations, seems to have given the first hint upon the subject: witness the beautiful and accurate impressions of Plants to be seen in the coal-formations." Although we may not know the exact moment that someone decided to decorate cloth or paper with the inked impressions of a leaf, bark, fish, or other natural textures, we do know that even great artists like Leonardo da Vinci were intrigued by nature printing, as a description of the process appears in his 15th century notes.

Spraying the painted leaves before printing gives them texture. After the print dried, the shapes' edges and the background areas were enhanced with textile markers and brush painting to create a beautiful watercolor-like print. By Betty Auchard.

LEAF PRINTING

Knowing a leaf's shape, vein pattern, or edge variation was crucial to early food gatherers. To survive, each generation relied on the experience of their elders and their own acute observation skills to identify whether a plant was edible or poisonous. Still, the eyes could be fooled, and the memory was often unreliable. A nature print taken directly from the plant, however, could be trusted.

In America in the 1700's, early prints were probably made by holding a leaf over a candle flame or a lamp until it was coated with a thick layer of black soot. Then when it was placed between two sheets of paper and rubbed, the plant's blackened image would transfer to the paper. It was Benjamin Franklin that Robert Little credits with an ingenious use of the process in 1739. Noting that the individual characteristics of a leaf impression were difficult to copy precisely, he used nature prints to foil counterfeiters. Franklin printed "three blackberry leaves on a sprig and a willow leaf with stipules" on Colonial currency and then kept the method a secret. It wasn't until 1963, when an anonymous article was attributed to him, that he received credit for his cleverness.

Today, leaf or nature printing is done mainly for artistic reasons. After your first print, you'll find it easy to understand why so many generations have found the process fascinating. I know that printing has changed the way I view leaves. I used to be drawn mainly to a leaf's color, especially in the fall. But now, I notice everything about a leaf—its outline, vein structure, even insect holes. As much as I enjoy this increased awareness, it has made walking around the block a very slow endeavor. I have to stop and start many times to examine leaves for good printing qualities. My neighbors would probably find it amusing if I told them that I covet their leaves more than their beautiful homes. But perhaps they know already, as I have made a lot of new friends as a trespasser.

Betty Auchard painted Inkodyes (see page 62) on an assortment of plant materials and overlapped the individual images to create a bouquet composition. The first leaf was left in place on the fabric to act as a mask as the second leaf was printed over it, and so on.

Collecting Leaves

Whether walking through a park, the woods, or your own backyard, nature offers many leaf printing options. Start by selecting leaves that have a pronounced vein pattern and are likely to be tough enough to withstand the printing process (oak, maple, fig). For the plant's sake, collect only as many fresh leaves as you can print in a day, as they tend to go limp or curl unless kept in the refrigerator in a plastic bag. Although summer will yield the largest selection, even winter leaves found under the snow can be washed and used to produce reasonably good prints.

Gold Lumiere metallic paint on black silk.

When traveling, many leaves will keep if you sandwich them between the pages of a book or magazine. This will keep them flat and protected until you arrive home. Don't wait too long to print, however, as they may mildew or become brittle.

Leaf Printing with Fabric Paints

Although thickened dyes can be used, fabric paints will catch more of the leaf's details. Select paint that isn't too thin, but has a thick creamy consistency. Make a test print; if the paint beads up on the leaf, clean the leaf with glass cleaner and try again or select a less glossy leaf.

A smooth, finely woven fabric (natural or synthetic fibers) whose texture will not interfere with the delicate leaf lines works best. A white or pastel colored fabric catches details best, but deep-toned colors or hand-dyed fabrics can make wonderful printing grounds if opaque or metallic paints are used. Before beginning to print, play with different leaf arrangements on your fabric so you'll have an idea of your desired design.

In the following demonstration, you'll learn the basic leaf-printing process that can be used on any fabric. However, to make learning the process more fun, we'll print with luscious metallic fabric paints on a jewel-toned Thai Silks habotai scarf. When you've finished the project, you'll have a beautiful hand-printed scarf to wear.

I Lay the leaf, backside up, on the telephone book page. Hold the stem and gently roll the metallic paint onto its surface. Coat it several times, but not so heavily that the paint pools around the veins. Use one color or mixtures of two colors.

Supplies
- Fresh leaves
- Habotai scarf (12" x 60" in royal purple, red, or black)
- Lumieré metallic paint (gold, super copper, olive)
- Masking tape
- Small foam roller
- Styrofoam tray palette
- Telephone book pages
- Tissue paper (cut slightly larger than leaves)

2 Lift the leaf by the stem (or with tweezers if the complete stem has been painted) and place the painted leaf face down on the fabric.

3 Cover the leaf with tissue paper, hold the leaf in place with one hand, and gently rub the leaf's surface with the other hand to transfer the impression. Avoid returning to a section you have already rubbed, as the leaf's placement may have shifted.

4 Remove the tissue paper, then carefully lift the leaf off the fabric by its stem. Continue this process until your leaf becomes worn. Then select a new leaf.

When printing over a dyed background, black ink is the best choice.

Sometimes leaf prints almost resemble etchings or lithographic prints because of their fine detail.

White and silver leaf prints on a black silk scarf by Carolyn A. Dahl.

Supermarkets offer a variety of fruits, vegetables, and leaves to print. Pineapple, grapefruit, leaf prints enhanced with textile markers by Carolyn A. Dahl.

FISH PRINTING AND GYOTAKU

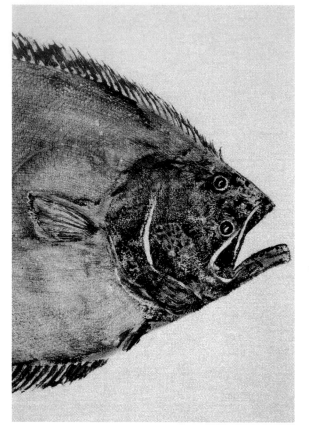

At one time or another, fish have entered our lives as food, symbols, or a source of artistic inspiration. What better way to honor and remember their bounty and beauty than through a fish print.

Even though I had files bulging with colorful fish photos, I had never thought about printing directly from fish until I met Winnie Lindveit. I was teaching a silk painting workshop, and Winnie invited me to dinner and to see her art work.

I've always loved the moment just before I enter the home of someone I don't know well. Sometimes the door opens to a house that could be anyone's, but at Winnie's, it opened to her passion—the sea. Everywhere I looked, the sea seemed close by. Shells, coral chunks, crab claws filled shoe boxes stacked three high on her studio shelves. Watercolor seascapes decorated the living room and fish identification

charts hung on doors. In the dining room I was treated to a full gallery of fish prints, some framed and others lying in stacks on the table like an art fish market.

That evening I learned about fish printing, and the differences in techniques. Winnie, like most fish printers in the West, prefers the direct printing method. The paint is applied to the fish, the fabric (or paper) is laid over it, and then the shape is transferred to the underside of the fabric by rubbing. Those who follow the Oriental, or indirect method, lay the fabric over a clean fish, and then dab the color onto the fabric to reveal the textured fish image; this is much like a stone rubbing. Not only can fish be printed with these two methods, but also seashells, seaweed, and other objects from the sea.

I returned to the hotel that night with more than memories of a delicious meal. I had a new process swimming in my head, two fish prints I traded for silk, a handful of perfect sand dollars, and more than a touch of Winnie's passion. Hoping she will inspire you, here's her process for direct fish printing on fabric.

Direct Fish Printing Method

Go fishing. Select a beautiful spot and contemplate nature until the fish that wants to be printed arrives. Or, purchase a fresh fish, with scales intact, at the market. Bass, flounder, and perch are good beginners' fish. Although many printers simply clean and print the fish intact, Winnie prefers to remove the insides, including the gills, to prevent moisture leakage during printing. Stuff the cavity

with paper towels to create volume. Sew the opening closed with a curved needle with thread that is doubled. Make the stitches unobtrusive and maintain a smooth belly line. Apply gentle pressure so any remaining moisture inside the fish will be released. Blot the outside of the fish with paper towels to clean and dry the surface. Lay the fish on wax paper placed on a table or counter.

The fabric requirements are the same as with leaf printing (smooth , light-colored or hand-dyed, wrinkle-free, any content) and the paint can be the same type.

Level and steady the fish by placing supports (modeling clay) under the tail, fins, and mouth. When all parts of the fish are level, lift the tail, fins, and head just enough to slip in a piece of scrap paper on top of the supports to protect the supports from paint. Return the parts to their former position. This scrap paper will need to be changed for every print you make.

If a centered image is desired, determine the center of the fish with a measuring tape. Draw vertical and horizontal center lines (on the wax paper) extending out from the fish. Cut the fabric into a rectangle slightly larger than the fish. Find the fabric's center by folding the fabric in half. Lay the fabric aside.

Prepare your printing colors. Dark colors give the best definition (black, navy, brown). Fabric paints work well, however, Winnie prefers one part artist's acrylic paint to one part acrylic gel medium, diluted slightly with water until a thick painting consistency is reached. Dab the paint onto the body of the fish using a foam brush. Work quickly, apply the paint in the direction of the scales. Do not paint over the eye, which will be painted in after the print is dry. Switch to a blender brush (fan-shaped) and paint the fins and tail. More than one color can be used and glitter can be added to give an iridescent effect. After the fish has been painted, lift the parts resting on the clay supports, and carefully remove the paint-soiled scrap paper before printing.

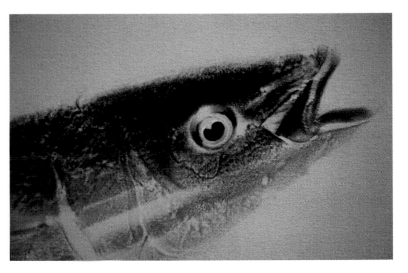

Match the fabric's fold line with those drawn on the wax paper. Carefully unfold the fabric and cover the fish, avoiding wrinkles or air bubbles. Gently press the fabric onto the fins, tail, belly, and head to anchor it. Begin in the center of the body and slowly rub with your hand toward the edges to transfer the paint to the fabric. Then proceed to the fins, tail, and lastly, the head. If necessary repeat the process, but be sure the fabric doesn't shift or the image will be blurred. Lift the fabric off the fish slowly, beginning with the head. Lay the print aside to dry. To make more prints, repeat the procedure. Experiment with varying the placement and colors, or adding water elements to the background. The fish may need to be cleaned about every third print to prevent paint buildup.

When the prints are finished, "life" must be returned to the fish by painting in the eye. Because the eye was not painted, it will appear as a blank circle. Once you paint the eye, the fish regains its spirit. As Winnie says "a good eye equals a good print." After the paint is dry, the fabric should be heat set according to the manufacturer's instructions.

If instead of painting an eye, you'd like a sparkly, dimensional, stick-on eye for your print, holographic molded fish eyes (used in real fish lures and similar to the disks decorating the Flying Fish Kimono quilt, page 8) are available from WTP Inc.

Study the eyes of fish closely before painting. Notice the large pupil banded by a ring of color, with a white highlight on this luminescent rainbow runner fish. Japanese oil paint on China silk, indirect method. Print by Ann Bae Machado.

Ann Bae Machado lives in Hawaii. When she goes for her daily swim, she often sees these beautiful flying gurnard fish leap out of the ocean and glide. Japanese oil paints on Oriental paper, indirect method. Print by Ann Bae Machado.

Indirect Fish Printing Method

In Japan, the direct method of fish printing is also used, but mainly for advertising purposes. A fishing tackle store owner might decorate banners with prints done in the direct method, or sell a kit containing rub-on carbon paper for the do-it-yourself fisherman.[2] But to be a true art form, worthy of the name gyotaku (fish rubbing), a print would need to be made by the indirect method (this attitude is starting to change however).

Supposedly invented by samurai warriors sometime in the Tokugawa Era (1600 to 1868), gyotaku proved not only their fishing abilities, but also their artistic capabilities. Both were required of a true samurai warrior. Few Japanese practice gyotaku today, but the numbers are growing internationally as skilled teachers revive the art form both in the East and West.[3]

Although thin Oriental paper is traditionally used, the indirect method also works on smooth silk such as habotai, or China silk. Water-based fabric paint may be used, but many artists prefer paints with an oil base. The fish is cleaned and prepared but is not painted as in the direct method, which is why some people claim that the fish can be eaten after a quick printing session (I don't recommend this). Instead, fabric (or paper) is laid over the fish and color tapped onto the fabric with a dauber (also called a tampo) in a delicate up and down motion.

A dauber is made from a square piece of silk, filled with cotton, gathered and closed with rub-ber bands. It should feel as soft as an earlobe. It takes some practice to achieve the right pressure, but because the image appears on top of the fabric like a rubbing, you can see the results immediately. Overlapping fish images are easier to achieve with the indirect method also as you can visually gauge their placement.

A print of a fish honors not only its life but all life. Fish printers know that the availability of beautiful fish requires a healthy environment and a respect for the species' survival. Many printers are reluctant to kill fish, especially female ones. Some printers, I've heard, even try to print from live fish. Supposedly, a fish can live out of water for a short time period. If one is quick and tenacious, fish can be painted, printed, cleaned, and returned to the water unharmed, or so I've heard. Although I have never seen these prints, I can't imagine a fish cooperating. However, I'm sure that the result of this struggle has an in-motion beauty all its own, and the process certainly deserves admiration.

Sometimes a good printing fish is kept for years by devoted printers who make hundreds of prints from that one specimen. If the fish is wrapped in plastic carefully, with the delicate fins and tails folded in, it can be frozen. When more prints are wanted, the fish is thawed, printed, cleaned, and returned to the freezer as quickly as possible. In fact, some printers confess shyly that the same fish has lived in their freezers for as long as six to eight years. These fish lovers feel it's much better to preserve a beautiful specimen than to go through many fish trying to find the same bold scale pattern or graceful tail shape.

If you've already eaten your fish, you can still make a bone print. Acrylic paint on cotton, direct method. Print by Winnie Lindveit.

FISH PRINT STAMPS

Another option is the one artist Fred Mullett uses. He makes a mold of a real fish from household silicone caulking, and then a plaster cast from the mold. Not only do the casts reduce the number of fish used but also offer other advantages. They retain the details of the original fish, are always ready to use, never acquire an odor, and can be remade if broken. From these casts, Fred makes numerous fish prints on paper using oil-based inks. Best of all, he has translated his prints into rubber stamps. So if you prefer not to work directly from a fish, you can use fabric paints or heat-transfer inks (page 88) with his fish stamps and still have the delicate beauty of an original fish print on your fabric.

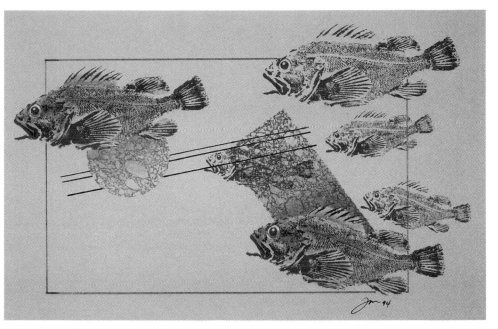

A sense of depth is created in this composition by changing the stamp size, varying the colors, and placing the fish in front of the sponged shapes. Print by Fred Mullett.

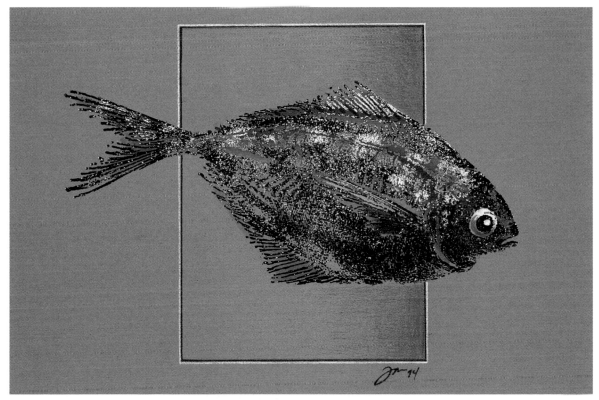

A rubber stamped image of a fish print has been embellished with color and details. Print by Fred Mullett.

Hand-painted and marbled silk give a watery background to the rubber stamped fish prints. Big rockfish and big finger mullet stamps © Fred Mullett Co.

After the fabric has been heat-set (according to manufacturer's instructions), many artists like to add a seal to their nature prints. Your name in Chinese characters can be carved into soapstone at many Chinese office supply stores. These hand-carved seals are used with the traditional vermilion paste (use with caution as it contains a poisonous mercury compound). You can also purchase rubber-stamp seals to use with red pigmented ink pads. Many of the designs in Chinese characters translate into beautiful sayings. Red Pearl Stamps offers some of my favorites: "First explore, then master, then create" and "Simplicity is the heart of elegance" and "In all things there is a natural truth."

SUN PRINTING (HELIOTROPIC)

Even though the July heat at noon could melt the smile off my face, I'm standing on a burning concrete driveway in full sun. At my feet, a mud-gray fabric begins its metamorphosis toward purple. As the gray edges tinge with pink, I'm fascinated again by the magic of sun-reactive, or heliotropic, dyes. By sensitizing the fabric with special dyes and then placing assorted objects on the fabric or folding sections of the cloth, I've blocked the sun's rays to create patterns. The process is a lot like getting a tan. Exposed parts of the skin (the sensitized fabric) change color, but the covered parts remain white.

Of course, the sun doesn't need me hovering over the fabric to do its work. But I'm reluctant to leave and miss any of the strange-hued color changes. So I bear the hot concrete just for the privilege of watching the pink fabric turn to lavender. Only when it ripens to a rich red-purple do I leave its side for a glass of iced tea.

A variety of sun-printed (heliotropic) fabrics.

Heliotropic Dyes

The dyes used to sensitize the fabric are called Inkodyes. Also known as sun-reactive or heliotropic dyes, they do not reveal their final color until exposed to sunlight or artificial ultraviolet light such as a sun lamp. Unlike the fiber-reactive class of dyes used in most of this book, Inkodyes are from a different class called vat dyes (the early fermentation process used old wine vats). They produce brilliant colors on untreated white or light color cellulose fibers (use on cotton, viscose rayon, and linen). The colors are very permanent and according to the supplier can "withstand strong soaps, boiling water, rubbing, dry-cleaning, common bleaches, or strong direct sunlight for a long time." [4]

Inkodyes are sold as a concentrated liquid that can be diluted with water or clear extender. In their light-proof plastic bottles, they can be stored in a cool, dark place for approximately one year with little color loss.

Color Mixing

Poured straight from the bottle, Inkodye resembles a grayish-white cream. This is its leuco form, from the Greek *leukos* meaning white. However, as soon as the dye makes contact with the air and light, it begins to change color. You don't have time to play around with color mixtures as you do with fiber-reactives, nor can you judge a color by sight. As the dyes don't show their true colors until exposed to light, fabric test strips have to be made beforehand. Then when you're ready to work, you can refer to your notes and mix the proportions quickly in a dim room.

Start by making test strips of all the stock colors. Inkodyes come in red, red-orange, orange, orange-yellow, yellow, yellow-green, green, blue-green, blue, blue-violet, violet, red-violet, brown, and black. The dyes are transparent so the undercolor will be affected by the applied color (blue dye over yellow fabric will produce a green color).

A mixture of one part dye to two parts water (or clear extender sold by manufacturer) will yield a medium shade. Dip or paint the dye onto a fabric strip and take it into full sun to develop. Keep notes on the proportions used, the exposure time, and fabric type. These can also be written on the fabric with permanent marker if you prefer.

Any object can be used for photograms as long as it can block the sun's rays.

If you find some of the colors too vivid, add a small amount of brown or black. If you want lighter shades (pastels), dilute the color with clear extender or with water. Adding the extender will maintain the dye's viscosity and minimize bleeding if the dye is used for stamping, stenciling, or printing. Water will dilute the dye's consistency but is a good choice for watercolor techniques, spraying, and immersing.

Photogram Process

Inkodyes can be used for many techniques: direct painting, printing, compression techniques, wax resist, and warp painting. But one of the most intriguing is making photograms in the sun. A photogram is a direct contact print made by laying opaque objects on fabric that has been sensitized by soaking in Inkodye. Where the object is placed, the sun will be blocked from reaching the light-sensitive fabric and little or no chemical reaction, or color change, will occur. When the cloth is dry and the objects are removed, their outlines will appear in the original

fabric color (or a modified one) to form the design. Those areas of the fabric not covered by an object will be exposed to the sunlight, causing the dye to react and the color to develop.

Many objects can be used to create patterns and shapes on fabric: lace, toothpicks, leaves, rocks, gutter screens, nursery plant trays, open net rug padding, opaque stencils, toys, precut cardboard and wood shapes, drafting templates, ribbon, twigs, and hand-cut stencils. Enlarged camera negatives may also be used, or you can make your own by drawing on Mylar or acetate with opaque inks.

You will need to create your design with the objects in a low light area (bathroom, garage) on a sturdy board (heavy cardboard, Masonite, foam board) and then bring the whole composition into the sun for developing (board must fit horizontally through doorway). You need to have enough interior light to work out your composi-

tion (plan it beforehand) but not enough to start your dyes reacting if you want strong color contrasts. Protect all work surfaces (counters, floors) with newspaper, as the dye stains.

It's important to choose a sunny day without clouds and an outdoor space that receives at least two hours of direct overhead sun—between 10:00 am and 2:00 pm is best. The temperature should be at least 65 degrees Fahrenheit for the dyes to develop properly. The development time varies with the climate but expect at least 20 to 30 minutes in direct overhead sun. For many geographical areas, this process will be limited to summer unless you use an artificial ultraviolet (UV) light, such as a sun lamp. The exposure time will be longer, however, and influenced by the age of the bulb, the distance from the work (12" to 24" is recommended), and the dye color you are using. Wear sunglasses to protect your eyes from the strong ultraviolet light.

BUTTERFLY DANCERS by Carolyn A. Dahl. The photogram design was embellished by adding texture with free motion machine stitching.

Photogram Process

In a semi-dark area, wearing your safety gear, pour the dye and water (1 to 2 ratio) into the container. Depending on your container and fabric size, 3" to 4" of solution should be enough for one yard. Cap the bottle immediately. Mix the solution well with the plastic spoon and submerge the fabric in the dye, pressing on the cloth to distribute the color evenly. Squeeze out excess dye solution so it won't pool or run on the board. Cover the dye container with the lid or a newspaper to block out light. The fabric is now sensitized and will react to light exposure.

Whenever I finish one batch of sun fabrics, I am always planning the next. The object box swells with new additions, the weather is watched, and I await the sun. During the year I studied art in Italy, I learned a word that so aptly describes my mood—*bramasole*. It means to long for, to desire, to yearn for the sun. Now I finally understand the Italian passion behind the word.

Supplies

- Assorted opaque objects
- Sturdy board
- Washed cellulose fabric (cut slightly smaller than board)
- Inkodyes
- Containers with lids for dyes—plastic, glass, or enamel only (Avoid large ones as they require too much dye.)
- Plastic measuring cups and spoons
- Weights to keep the objects from blowing off the fabric (rocks)
- Sheet of unscratched glass or Plexiglas for covering paper stencils or negatives
- Respirator, eye goggles, rubber gloves, and long-sleeved shirt

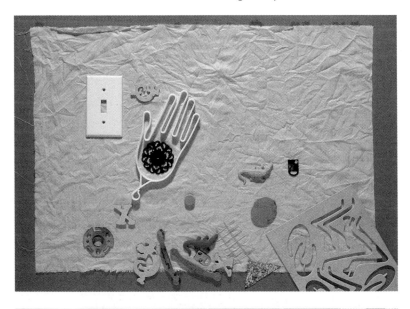

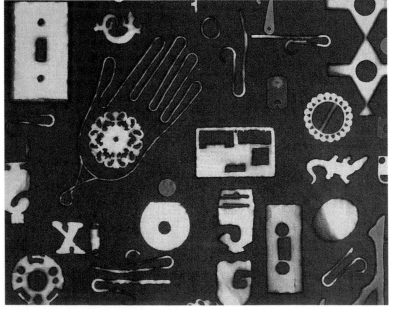

Lay the sensitized fabric on the board and smooth out wrinkles and folds. Begin arranging the objects on the fabric (if needed, add weights or a sheet of glass or Plexiglas). When you are pleased with the design, carefully carry the board horizontally into the sunlight.

The dyes will start to react immediately. Allow the fabric to dry completely in the sun. If you remove the objects or stencils while the fabric is still wet and in the sun, the once-covered areas will begin to develop. If you want to stop the color development, move the board to a dim area, remove the objects, and wash the fabric immediately.

After exposure to the sun, the dye is permanently fixed in the fabric and no additional heat setting is necessary. To remove the unreacted dye from the areas that weren't exposed to the sun, the fabric must be washed. Fill your machine with plenty of warm soapy water and wash on a regular cycle and machine dry. I have noticed that when I use blue in strong concentrations, it sometimes rubs off on the plastic parts of my dryer. Even though it has never transferred to subsequent loads, I prefer to line dry that color.

CHAPTER 6

Sponge and Moldable Foam Printing

YOU DRAW TO YOURSELF WHAT IS MOST IN YOUR MIND, according to folk wisdom. I guess sponges are planted in mine. Ever since I began collecting sponges for fabric printing, they have appeared all over my life.

I used to avoid the cleaning aisle in supermarkets, but now I'm fascinated by mop heads, bottle wands, squeegees, and cleaning sponges. At cosmetic counters, I purchase the newest eye-shadow applicators and sponge wedges, promising myself I'll wear more make up. When my local five-and-dime store owner digs into a pile of objects that hasn't been disturbed in years and pulls out a fanciful bee sponge, my day is made. The drawers fill and the cupboards bulge with my collection, but there's not a sponge in the house that anyone dares use for cleaning.

Still, as much as I enjoy adding each new sponge, its discovery always shocks me somewhat. I'm surprised at how long it took me to see all the sponge forms that I now know surround me. It's startling to think about how many other things reach out to me daily, but are never noticed because I haven't put the thought of them in my mind. So maybe the value of my collection goes beyond fabric decoration. Perhaps each sponge will remind me to look a little closer, and have a greater appreciation, for all the humble objects sharing my life.

EYE VEILS by Carolyn A. Dahl. Hand-painted and sponged cloth (triangle cellulose sponges, sea sponges), dispersed dye photo transfer, quilting, beads, marble texture stamp © Stampendous. Photo by Maria Davila.

ANIMAL/SEA SPONGES

When you print with a sea sponge, it's hard to believe that it is actually the remains of a primitive, multi-cellular animal. (Sponges are classified as animals because they eat their food by pumping water through their body cavities to extract nutrients; whereas, plants manufacture their own food.) These cavities are what account for its phylum being called *Porifera*, from the Latin word meaning pore-bearer. Sometimes the pores are more like channels producing a wave pattern on the cloth, reminiscent of the waves that used to wash through them. At other times, the pattern is delicate and feathery, like coral imprints. Sea sponges never let you forget the origin of their beauty, however, as they always drop a few grains of sand into your hand and smell faintly of the sea even after years of use.

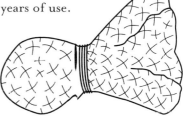

CELLULOSE SPONGES

Most of the cleaning sponges you will find are made from cellulose. Often called natural sponges, they are made from natural materials such as cotton or wood pulp, which manufacturers process into a fiber structure, the sponge. Because they are manufactured sponges, their pore patterns are more predictable and regular than sea sponge patterns. Although the pore shapes may not be as fluid looking, cellulose sponges offer other interesting options for fabric decoration.

Many cellulose sponges have ridges or waffle-patterned surfaces that are ready to print. Sponge cloth, a thin sheet sponge made to be used like a dishcloth, can be purchased in several textures. My favorite is a tire-track pattern. Cut the 6" by 7" sheet into smaller shapes, glue them onto a backing (wood, foam board), and you have a simple printing block for texture. The sheet sponge can also be gathered into a paint dauber for applying touches of pattern to backgrounds or other shapes.

Having a dense structure, cellulose sponges can be cut with scissors or an X-Acto knife into interesting shapes. Cellulose sponges also come in tightly compressed sheets (Design A Sponge) that expand on contact with water into full-sized sponges. Because the design is drawn on the dry sheet's surface and cut out while it is flat, more complex shapes can be created.

Place a small sponge inside a square of sponge cloth, gather the sides, and secure with a rubber band for a textured paint dauber.

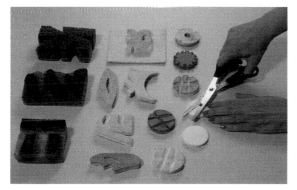

Sponges can be purchased with surface patterns or cut into interesting printing designs. Left to right: thick cellulose sponges with large sections removed, pop-up sponge sheets cut into abstract shapes, circular cosmetic sponges being cut with scissors.

An assortment of sponge-printed cloth. Top to bottom: Sea sponges form a flower design, sea sponges on wet fabric, blue loofah print with spiral stamp © All Night Media, star-shaped cosmetic sponges on tire track pattern (right), circle sponges with cut Oriental designs, and waffle-patterned sponge.

SYNTHETIC SPONGES

As the name implies, these sponges are made from synthetic materials, or chemical solutions. Their printing surfaces are finely textured with small air bubbles, or none at all. Synthetic sponges are the best choice when you want your sponged shape to obscure most of your background color or pattern, as they hold and deposit more colorant. Most synthetic sponges are sold in cosmetic, upholstery, children's, or craft stores. Children's departments yield wonderful animal shapes that can be used as purchased.

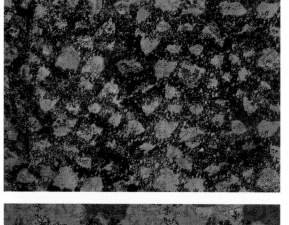

Sections of a cellulose sponge have been cut away so only small portions of the background fabric can be seen.

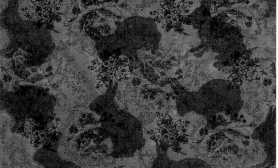

A rabbit-shaped sponge printed over the same hand-painted fabric as in previous photo.

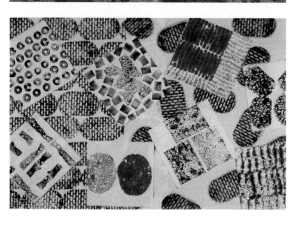

Some of the many patterns in my growing sponge collection. Notice how moisture in the cloth affects some designs.

Sponging Procedure: Animal, Cellulose, and Synthetic Sponges

Although sponging can be done with dyes, fabric paints (darker colors are best) give more definite textures. Select a smooth white fabric (or a hand-dyed fabric) and make a test print on both dry and wet fabric. The moisture content will affect the pattern as the water disperses the color.

The process of sponging is pretty simple. You can either sponge print the cloth in an all-over texture, or use the sponge like a stamp for individual prints. Either way the process is the same. Wet the sponge, squeeze out excess water, and lay it on a paper towel to drain slightly. Tape the fabric to a printing surface (doubled old sheet) to prevent shifting. Spread fabric paint in a thin layer (if it's too thick, spray with water) on a tray and press the sponge lightly into the color. Or you can paint the color on the sponge's surface if it is a cut or shaped sponge. Place the color-loaded sponge face down on the fabric and apply even, gentle pressure with the flat of your hand. If you press hard with your fingers, color blobs will appear on the fabric. If the sponge is shaped, press carefully around the edges to ensure it contacts the fabric.

Lift the sponge off the fabric slowly. Use your opposite hand to hold down the fabric. When you have finished printing, wash your sponges immediately in running water to remove color. Let the sponges dry before storing.

Explorations
- Overlap sponged images
- Paint multiple colors on one sponge
- Print one color on top of another
- Drag the sponge across the fabric
- Spray the print to bleed colors
- Print with a fabric resist, or bleach, instead of a colorant
- Sponge through plastic grids, open lace, stencils
- Print on a textured cloth

MOLDABLE FOAM PRINTING

MagicStamp® (also known as PenScore™) is a special moldable foam sponge that has a closed cell structure, thus no visible pores. It is a unique material because its surface can be softened with heat and impressed with a textured object. The cooled foam can then be painted and pressed to the cloth like any other sponge or stamp. If you want to change the pattern, just heat the foam again, and the pattern is erased.

MagicStamp® comes in three forms:

- The first is Bulk Block Stock (each block is $2\,^{3}/_{4}$" x $1\,^{1}/_{4}$") which is good for impressing small objects or lace details.

- The second is Sheet Stock, 8" x 10" sheets about $^{3}/_{8}$" thick. The sheets can be cut into shapes and mounted on wood or foam board or left uncut for flexible printing of larger objects, such as a crocheted baby dress.

- The third is a Geometric Block Set, composed of 10 precut shapes ($^{7}/_{8}$" thick) such as circles, triangles, and squares. Each piece can be used separately or as part of an interlocking design.

MagicStamp® can also be engraved by wetting the block or sheet slightly to prevent tearing and drawing into the surface with a ball point pen or pencil. These lines will not erase, however, as they are scratched into the surface.

Fabric printed with moldable foam blocks impressed with a potato masher and dishcloth.

MagicStamp® comes in three forms to match any project: blue Bulk Block Stock, Sheet Stock, and a Geometric Block set of interlocking shapes.

One of my favorite uses for moldable foam printing is to create memory cloth from the actual objects associated with the event. The only requirement is that the objects have some texture, an interesting outline, fit the chosen foam shape, and have an emotional importance to you (a baby dress, beaded appliqué from an old prom dress).

For instance, if I want to commemorate a special wedding, I can actually press sections of the wedding gown lace into the warm foam block and not worry about destroying the fabric. Moldable foam printing is a perfect technique to create one-of-a-kind gifts on cloth or paper: a wedding quilt for your daughter, a pillow for a friend's new home, a custom-made invitation to a shower or a baby's christening, or specially decorated pages for an avid memory book maker. Or it can be a gift to yourself, as in my memory quilt. Each object printed on the cloth will forever remind me of a special visit home, the beautiful moments with family, the storybook dolls in my old upstairs bedroom, and the funny stories I don't ever want to forget.

Supplies

- Objects to impress
- MagicStamp® blocks (or sheets)
- 300 to 400 degree Fahrenheit heat source (heat gun, iron, hot plate)
- Rubber gloves to protect hands from heat
- Black water-based fabric paint (thick cream consistency)
- Plastic plate for paint palette
- Small foam roller
- White fabric (any content) or paper

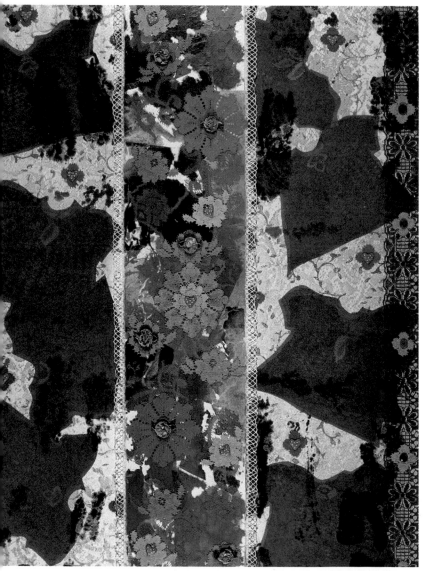

FOR HUNTER ROSE AND ALL THE CHILDREN by Carolyn A. Dahl. Hand-dyed and painted fabric and lace, porcelain hearts, MagicStamp® prints from my baby dress crocheted by my mother.

Printing blocks impressed with pasta can be a wonderful reminder of a special dinner. Fabric by Carolyn A. Dahl. Assembly by Margaret Sindelar.

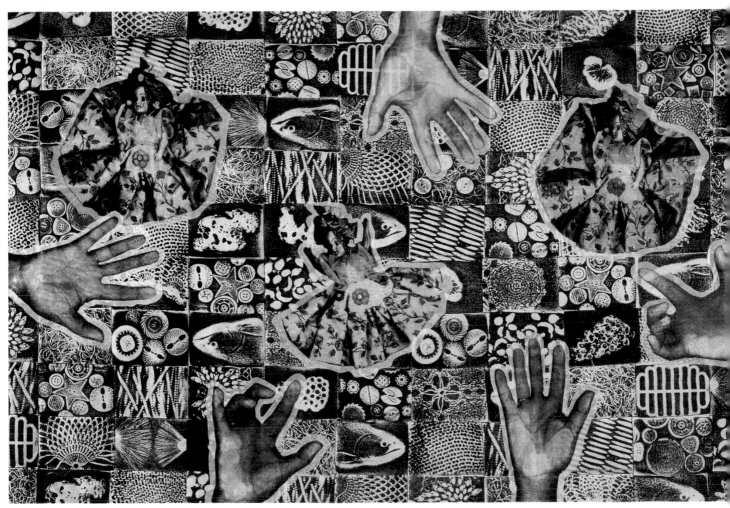

DON'T THROW AWAY MY DOLLS by Carolyn A. Dahl. My memory quilt documents a visit with my family and was printed with blocks impressed with grandmother's buttons, mother's crochet work, my sister's dishcloth (we cooked our favorite dishes), sea coral from a recent Florida trip, and fused images of my hands reaching for my storybook dolls just as I try to catch and hold my memories.

MagicStamp® Step-by-Step

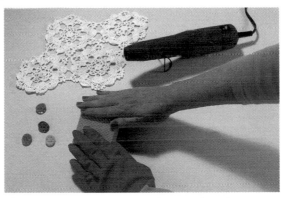

1 Hold the MagicStamp® block 4" to 6" away from the heat source for approximately 20 to 30 seconds. Keep the block or heat gun moving to prevent scorching. Full sheets require more time to heat the total surface area.

2 When the surface looks moist, immediately press the warm foam over the object and hold firmly for about 10 to 25 seconds. If using a piece of sheet stock, place a large book over the object and foam to help distribute the pressure.

3 Lift the block off the object; its texture and shape will be recorded in the foam. Create blocks from all your objects before you begin printing.

4 Place fabric on work surface and smooth out wrinkles. Using foam roller, apply fabric paint to the block.

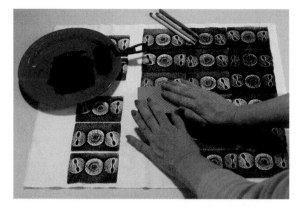

5 Press the block to the cloth making sure the edges contact the fabric. When you've finished printing, wash the block with water and mild soap (do not use a toothbrush to remove paint as it will scratch surface). When the paints have dried, the images may be painted, embellished, or colored with colored pencils. Heat set your fabric paints according to manufacturer's instructions.

6 Each foam block used to print the fabric for my memory quilt brings back a special moment during my visit with my family.

The largest sponge I ever had in my collection was my Space Sponge. I dyed a van load of scrap upholstery foam to create this 4-foot x 6-foot bundle for an outdoor art festival (it was later sold to a museum). In contrast, the smallest sponge in my collection is only ⅜" long. It came from my eye. I was teaching a workshop called Sponging on Handwovens at a national weavers' conference and my parting words to my students were: "You never know where sponges will turn up in your life." Little did I suspect that two days later, one would be stitched to my eye during emergency surgery for a retinal detachment. As it later had to be removed, it is now the most treasured part of my collection—the sponge that saved my eyesight.

Detail of finished memory quilt DON'T THROW AWAY MY DOLLS by Carolyn A. Dahl.

CHAPTER SEVEN

Compression Dyeing

HAVE YOU EVER TIE-DYED A T-SHIRT, pulling up the fabric into a peak and wrapping it round and round with string? If so, you have used a compression dyeing technique. Although most people think that tie dyeing originated in the 1960's, it is actually one of the numerous compression techniques that have been used for centuries by many cultures.

In compression dyeing, the flat fabric is manipulated into planned wrinkles through braiding, knotting, twisting, pleating, scrunching, folding, gathering, stitching. To maintain its 3-D shape during the dyeing process, the compressed cloth is sometimes further secured with bindings (string, rubber bands, clamps). The ready-to-dye fabric is often quite beautiful, like small sculptures. It may resemble an origami bird, be covered in a fringe of colored threads, or gathered like waves lapping the shore line. But each shape has a purpose: it blocks, channels, or admits the dye into the creases. The tightly compressed wrinkles force the dye to distribute the color load differently as it dries, thereby creating different patterns on the fabric.

Even though this method of dyeing is centuries old, few countries have given names to individual patterns, except the Japanese (white shadow, meandering stream pattern, wood grain). Perhaps you've heard the Japanese word Shibori? It refers to the complete body of compression (or shape-resisted) techniques. Shibori has no English equivalent, but

continued

SHIBORI STORM by Carolyn A. Dahl. Compression dyed (binding, pleating and scrunching) silk. Photograph by Charlotte Cosgrove and Helen Orman.

according to the authors of the book SHIBORI, "the word comes from the verb root shiboru , 'to wring, squeeze, press' ... the word emphasizes the action performed on the cloth, the process of manipulating fabric."[1]

That's a definition to remember because the physical action is the key to the technique's beauty. It is also the way to read the fabric. With experience, it is possible to look at compression dyed cloth and mentally reconstruct its former dimensional shape. Within the finished pattern, the action of the dyer's hands can always be traced because the cloth never forgets.

Sometimes, however, as in very old Japanese Shibori fabrics, the patterns are so complex that they cannot be understood or reproduced immediately. I'm glad they can't. For as long as dyers are intrigued with the puzzles left in these old textiles, the better the chances that the techniques will survive and be passed on to the next set of hands.

Dyeing Procedure

In traditional methods of compression dyeing, the fabric is immersed in dye, usually Indigo (a vat dye) which coats the fibers a deep blue. As we will be using a direct application method (painting on the dye) and a different class of dyes (fiber-reactive dyes), the results will vary slightly from those achieved with traditional immersion techniques.

Fiber-reactive dyes crawl more than vat dyes and may migrate under bindings to obliterate some patterns, so it's important to thicken your dyes (page 25) to slow their progress through the fabric folds and to create crisper shapes. After you've compressed your fabric using any of the chapter's techniques, follow the painting procedure below using thickened MX dyes.

1 Immerse the fabric in water, squeeze out the excess moisture, allow fabric to drain on a towel. Wetting the cloth will drive out the air molecules filling the capillary spaces of the dry fabric and allow the liquid dye to be absorbed more readily (if you wet the fabric first to make the compression process easier to execute, you can skip this step).

2 Prepare thickened fiber-reactive dyes. Mix your colors fairly strong as the wet fabric will dilute the intensity. It's impossible to predict exactly how thick a dye paste should be as each cloth will absorb differently. But I usually mix the first color I plan to apply to the fabric the thinnest so it will penetrate deeper into the folds. Then the following colors can vary, reserving the thickest paste for the last application and for areas in which I don't want the dye to spread very much.

Also, in general, dye penetrates fabric more easily when (a) the fabric is lightweight and has a smooth surface, (b) the fabric is compressed

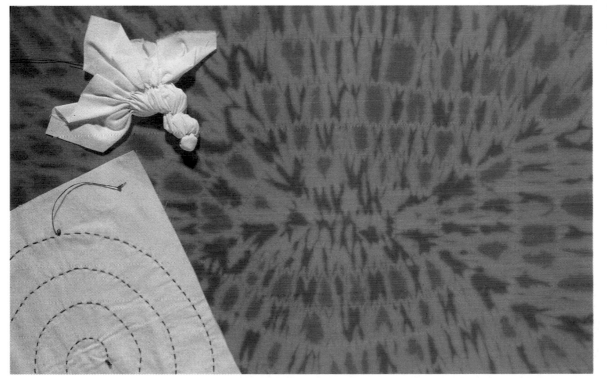

The three stages of a compression dyed fabric.

Mary Ann Willey immersed her stitched and gathered cotton fabric in an Indigo dye bath.

After the compressed fabric is painted with dye, it must remain in its dimensional form as it dries.

loosely, (c) the fabric is wet, and (d) the dye paste is thin. Thus, if your finished fabric has too many white, undyed areas, you may need to thin your dye or wet the fabric more so the color will spread deeper into the folds. If, however, the resulting pattern is weak with all the colors blurred together, you need to increase your compression tension and use a thicker dye paste so it won't migrate so far.

3 Activate the thickened dye (or presoak the compressed fabric in soda ash solution, page 25). Lay the fabric on plastic. Wearing rubber gloves, paint on the dyes with a brush or foam applicator using some of the techniques suggested under the compression methods. Stop painting before you feel you're finished. Remember, the dye will continue to blend long after you stop adding color.

4 Cover the fabric with plastic and allow it to dry overnight in its compressed dimensional shape. Resist the temptation to untie or open up the folds to peek. Uncover the fabric the next day and allow it to air dry. If the dimensional shape is undone while the fabric is still wet, the dyes will bleed and your pattern will become less defined, or perhaps lost entirely. Some very large pieces will take two to three days to dry.

5 If the fabric is allowed to dry slowly, the MX series of dyes will have batch set. Rinse the dry, still compressed fabric to remove excess dye before undoing bindings, stitches, knots, etc. (This eliminates colored fingers.) Then wash the cloth according to the fabric content.

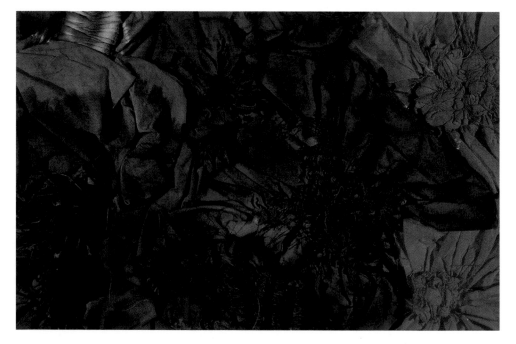

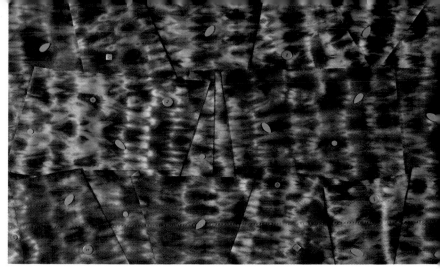

BRAIDING

Anyone who ever wore braids as a child knows firsthand what a compression technique feels like. My scalp still tingles remembering the pulling and tugging as great handfuls of hair disappeared into skinny little whips. Now, whenever I braid fabric, I feel a special empathy for the cloth. After all, it's the only surface design technique I've ever tried on my own body.

1 Cut washed fabric (white or light-colored cotton, silk, or rayon) into three equal strips approximately 6" to 8" wide. A greater width can be used, but the dye will be less likely to reach the innermost folds. The length of the strips should be approximately 1 to 1¼ yards long.

2 Wrap a rubber band several times around the three strips, about 1½" from the top end. Slip one loop of the band over the doorknob of a closed door and begin braiding. Don't worry about how the material is folding, just maintain an even tension. Secure the finished braid end with another rubber band.

3 When painting the braid, think about its four sides: the top, the bottom, the right side, and the left side. Because the cloth strips have been interlaced, each strand will appear on the top surface, disappear to the bottom, come around the sides, and reappear on top again. Thus, if red dye is painted across the top of the braid, only the fabric strips that happen to be on top at that time will receive the color. Also, just as many individual hairs make up each hair braid, many fabric folds make up each strand of the cloth. Thus the red dye would also only make contact with those fabric creases facing outward on the braid. Experiment with different ways to paint the braid.

- Paint the top of the braid one color, the bottom another, and the two sides a third color.
- Paint a light color on the top and side surfaces. Turn the braid over and paint the former bottom surface a dark color. Leave the braid in this position to dry. The dark color will migrate down into the lighter areas.
- Paint bands of one color around the circumference of a braid, spaced ½" to 1"

apart along its length. Select a color that was mixed with several other colors. The moisture in the braid will pull the individual colors out of the painted bands and into the white areas.

- Paint bands of alternating colors several inches apart. Allow the colors to bleed together.
- Using a fan-shaped blending brush, lightly drag one color of dye across the four sides of the braid. Barely touch the surface, leaving a trail of irregular lines. Repeat with a second, then a third color. The final effect will be a spotty pattern against a mostly white background.
- Re-braid an already painted braid and add new colors.

If a braid is painted, re-braided and painted again, many rich colors can be achieved.

Experiment with the many ways dye can be painted on a braid.

Diagram of three-strand and four-strand braiding.

TWISTING

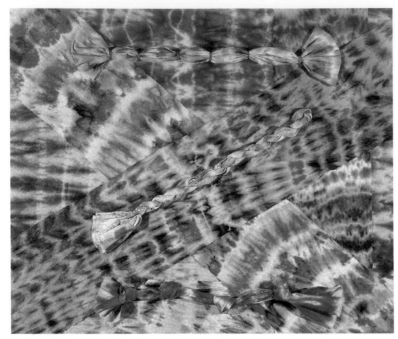

fabric first makes it easier to twist) in each hand. Begin twisting until the fabric curls back on itself. Wrap a rubber band around the two ends to secure the twist. If the twist goes slack in the center, you may need to tie a string around that area, or wrap the twisted fabric around a cardboard tube and secure. Twisted fabric can be painted with the same methods as the braids.

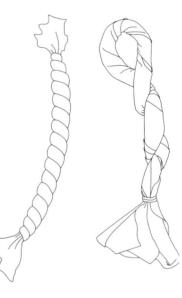

Twist fabric until it curls back on itself. Twist will relax slightly.

Examples of fabrics that were knotted, twisted, and bound before dyeing.

The action of twisting fabric forms soft folds that resist the dye only slightly. Because the dye is able to move further into the inner folds of the fabric, wider pieces of cloth may be used. Hold one end of a piece of wet fabric (wetting the

KNOTTING

In this technique, compression occurs only at intervals where a knot is made, leaving much of the fabric loosely gathered and able to receive dye freely. You can pull up sections of a flat piece of fabric and make random knots, or you can place knots along the length of a slightly gathered fabric. The knots must be tight enough to block some of the dye, but loose enough to be untied later. To paint, apply a color or many colors on or around the knots and then a different color on the unknotted areas. Sometimes interesting effects happen if you hang or drape the fabric so the dyes will bleed in one direction.

Loosely gather fabric and make knots along the length.

BINDING

First pleat (or loosely gather) the wet fabric to reduce its bulk (up to 24" wide fabric can be gathered and dyed successfully). Place rubber bands around the top and bottom ends to hold the pleats in place. Then add additional bindings (rubber bands, twist ties, dental floss, string) along the pleated fabric at intervals of approximately 2" to 3", or in spiral or crisscross patterns across the length. Paint the fabric with the dyes in a similar technique to braiding and knotting. Not only will the creases cause a pattern but so will the bindings where they cross the fabric and block the

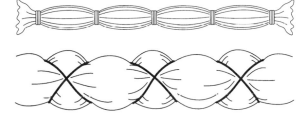

Bind the fabric at intervals

dye (see definite string lines in a bound discharged fabric on page 114). A variation of this dyeing technique is to bind an already dyed cloth and paint selected bumps with metallic fabric paint.

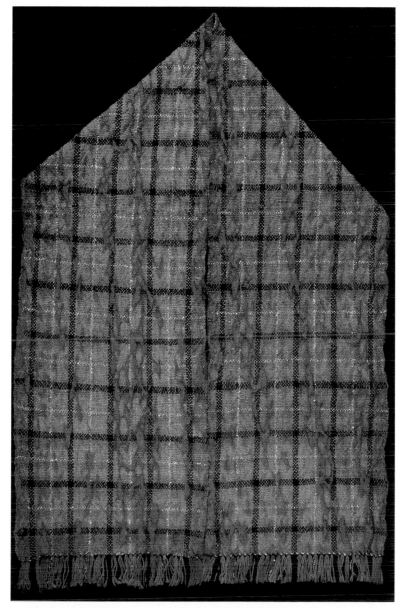

Metallic paint highlights the dimensional character of handwoven compressed fabric. Scarf dyed by the author, woven by Connie Elliott.

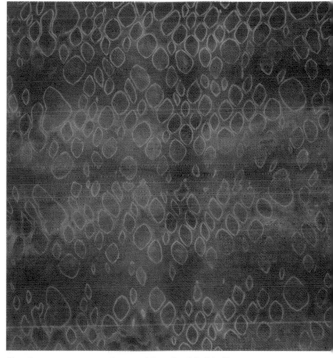

Circular patterns are best achieved with binding techniques on silk chiffon.

SCRUNCHING

The random pattern produced by this method gives a mottled or marbled effect. The wet fabric can be scrunched on a piece of cardboard and slightly thickened dye poured, painted, or dripped over it. Slanting the board can also affect the pattern.

Or the fabric can be compressed into a bundle that is wrapped tightly with rubber bands or strings, or stuffed into a nylon stocking, or packed into a small glass jar for dyeing. Once dry, the fabric can be opened up, re-scrunched, and dyed again if desired. (See title page for finished fabric.)

Scrunch the fabric into a ball and bind it with string or rubber bands.

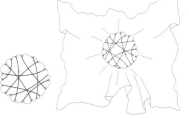

SILK ENSEMBLE by Carolyn A. Dahl. Silk fabric dyed with the compression technique of scrunching.

Pouring the dye into the folds of a scrunched fabric on a slanted board creates interesting patterns.

FOLDING AND PLEATING

This technique is especially beautiful on silk. Compress the fabric into regular or irregular pleats or folds. Work across the fabric width, on the diagonal, or make up your own pleating method. For crisper lines, iron the edges of the silk. When painting, experiment with different techniques: apply dye to one edge and allow it to migrate into the inner folds, paint different colors on each edge, open some pleats and pour in dye, use very thin and very thick dye, or substitute diluted fabric paint for the dye. Do not unpleat the fabric until the dye or paint is absolutely dry.

EARTH STRATA #1 by Carolyn A. Dahl. Pleated silk fabric, fabric paint. Photo by Mike McCormick.

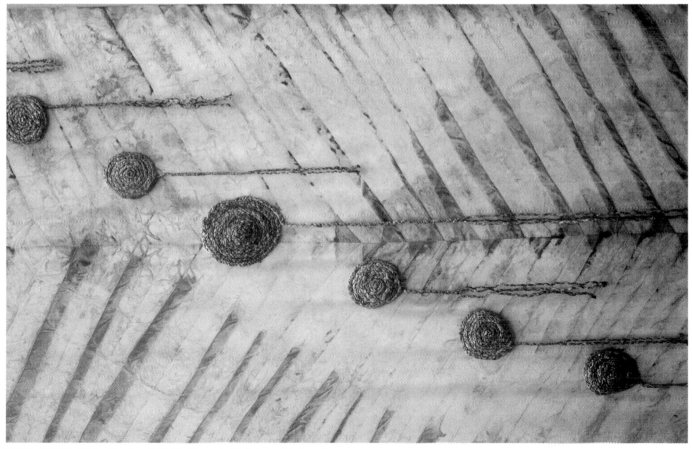

EARTH STRATA #2 by Carolyn A. Dahl. Pleated silk fabric, fabric paint.

STITCHING

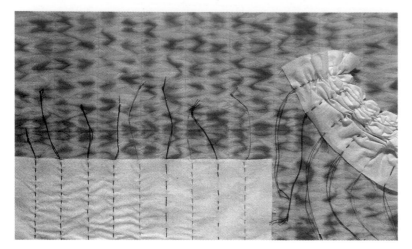

Closely spaced rows of running stitches create a wood grain pattern on the cloth.

Hotel sewing kits. I can't resist them. I leave the shower cap in its plastic, ignore the shampoo, use half of the lotion, but always take the kit with me. Why do I want it? A few bands of thread, a white button or two, a needle, a tiny pair of scissors tucked into a matchbook. These are hardly coveted materials. But I'm a textile artist. I claim thread and collect my tools wherever I find them—no matter their actual worth. The scissors may be almost useless, the button plain, the thread boring, but they are my life's symbols with value beyond function. I have to tuck them in my suitcase and fly them home.

What is it about stitching that so fascinates me? A needle pierces the cloth and pulls a colored thread along behind it. But something in that broken, in-and-out, dot-to-dot line appeals and satisfies. My eye can follow the thread for hours as batting gets stitched to quilts, buttons to blouses, sleeves to coats, and sequins to gowns.

Yet stitching intrigues me for another reason. So many times as I've ripped out a misplaced row of stitches, or removed an appliquéd fabric shape, I've been captivated by the beauty of the empty hole pattern. Like little bird feet walking across the cloth, the tracks of the removed thread invite my eye to follow. Perhaps these phantom stitches are why the stitch-and-dye compression method is one of my favorites: the pattern is caused by stitches but the design isn't revealed until the stitches are removed.

Instead of braiding or binding the fabric, stitches are pulled into tight gathers which resist the dye. In Indonesia, the method is called *Tritik*, or stitch resist. Unlike other compression techniques, which yield more textural designs, stitching can be used to achieve definite shapes, such as flowers or leaves.

This method also has another plus—it's portable. I have often envied needlepointers working away in airports, making use of their waiting time. So many of my dyeing and painting techniques require the materials of a full studio. But now I, too, can work while I travel, undisturbed by anyone because they think they know what I'm doing. However, when I suddenly pull up my quilting design into a lumpy, gathered mass, I do get puzzled looks, and sometimes seat changing.

Still, the stitch-and-gather method is the perfect travel companion. Even if I've forgotten my materials at home, and the creative urge strikes in some lonely hotel room, I can always turn to the handy little sewing kit just a bathroom away. It works just fine to stitch designs into any number of things in my suitcase.

Besides, it's kind of comforting. Every other item in the room feels anonymous. But a sewing

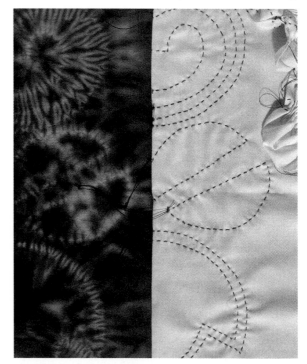

The fabric is folded in half and the design is stitched through both layers for a mirror image effect.

kit makes you feel at home. I worry, though, that its days in the gift basket are numbered. We need to show management that its kits are still noticed by its guests. So if you find one, use it or take it home. We don't want the hotel sewing kit to become another "remember when" item in our culture.

Stitching Process

1 Select a closely-woven, smooth fabric for stitch-and-dye patterns (open weaves will also create interesting, although less precise designs). The design can be stitched on a single layer of cloth, but if it is done on folded cloth, several images or a mirror image will result depending on how the design was traced on the fabric (see star stencil on page 85 also). With some very fine fabrics, such as a delicate silk, multiple layers can be stitched at one time.

2 Draw or trace the design on the fabric with a soft pencil (#2, or Ebony). The design can be as simple as a series of straight lines or more intricate like some quilt stencils. When choosing a design, remember that you must be able to pull up and gather each line or shape separately. So draw your pattern on paper first and mentally decide where each stitched line will begin and end.

3 Thread a large-eyed, sharp needle (crewel or embroidery) with a strong thread, doubled and knotted at the end so it won't pull through the hole left by the needle. The thread must be strong enough to withstand pulling without breaking and should suit the weight of the fabric. Thus a light-weight silk fabric would need a lighter weight thread such as doubled quilting thread; whereas, cotton or rayon fabric could be stitched with a thicker thread such as doubled carpet, home decorating, or upholstery thread. The thread can be long if your design is a straight line, but curves or

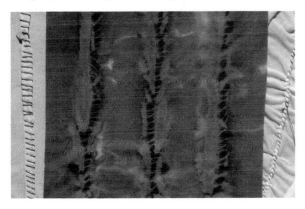

A finished mirror image design. Placing four stitched rows close together makes an interesting blossom texture.

complex shapes require shorter lengths of thread.

4 Sew along your design lines using a running stitch. An overcast stitch can also be used, but it is only done over the edge of a folded fabric. It's best to use a long needle for overcasting as the fabric collects on the needle as you go, and is then pushed back over the needle's eye onto the thread. The length of the running stitch can vary from small to medium to suit your design. A large stitch can be used for certain effects, but it will not resist the dye as well. Usually the stitching is done parallel to the weft so you don't have to work with long lengths of thread that may tangle. However, you can stitch in any direction, or place the rows close together or far apart, for the process to work.

5 Cut the thread, leaving a 2" to 3" tail at the end of the row or shape. Knot this end immediately so the thread doesn't slip out as you continue to stitch the remaining design.

6 Pull on the knotted threads to gather the fabric into tight folds when the stitched design is complete; you should not be able to see the thread between the folds. The amount of compression determines how much dye will penetrate the fabric. As this process can be very hard on the hands,

left:
Sections of the fabric were folded and the edges overcast. After gathering, very strong, thick dye was painted over the stitches to create dark areas.

After the stitch-
es are removed,
take a moment
to enjoy the
beautiful topog-
raphy of the
fabric.

ing and beautiful at this point
that I often wait weeks before I
proceed to the next step.
Finally, I reluctantly plunge the
bumpy fabric into soapy water
for its final wash and rinse. As I
iron it flat, however, I can still
see traces of its former dimensional self in the pattern and
tiny wrinkles.

Stitching From Stencils

Quilting stencils make excellent templates for
stitch-dyed designs. Most stencil designs can be
traced onto the fabric and stitched as is. Some,
however, will need to be modified slightly (see
flower stencil on page 85). Trace the stencil first
on paper and analyze the shape. If lines overlap or
are too close, if shapes run together and don't
form individual units, or if the line is too long to
gather, you will need to adjust the design. Taking
a little time to think through the process, and
marking the changes on paper first, will ensure
that the stencil you've selected will work well with
the stitch-and-dye method.

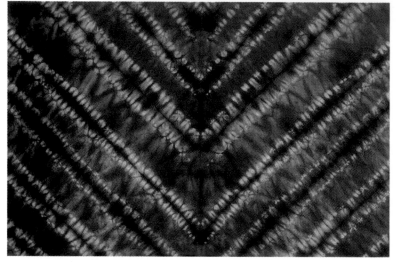

The stencil design can either be stitched on a
single layer of fabric or a folded fabric. Stitching
on one layer will result in a less defined stitched
design, but many wonderful fold patterns.
However, if one re-stitches over the lines during
quilting, the stitched pattern once again dominates the fold pattern.

If the stencil design is used on folded fabric,
only half of the design needs to be traced onto the
fabric, as the final result is a mirror image of the
design. Begin by folding the fabric in half. Lay the
stencil on the fabric with the fold line running
down the center of the stencil. Trace only half of
the stencil design onto the fabric. Remove the
stencil, connect any gaps in the lines, and pin the
fabric together so it will stay folded while stitching. Starting and ending at the fabric fold, stitch
over the half-design going through both layers.
Gather up the threads, and paint the bundle.
When opened and unfolded, the two sides of the
stencil design will join to form one shape.

The finished
stitch-dyed
fabric, even after
washing and
ironing, still
carries the mem-
ory of its former
dimensional
shape in the
pattern.

well-placed bandages can keep the thread from
cutting into your fingers.

7 Cut off the end knot of each thread and separate the doubled thread into two strands and
tie the ends into a tight knot to secure the gathers.
The fabric is now ready to be painted with dye.
Hint: Don't force the dye under the stitches by
dabbing with the brush too hard, or over saturat-
ing the fabric around the stitches.

8 Remove the stitches when the fabric is dry. Use
a small pair of scissors with thin blades. A
seam ripper will work, but be careful not to stab a
hole in the fabric. Proceed slowly, and use a good
light to help locate the threads and avoid cutting
the fabric. I find it easiest to clip off the knots
first. This releases the gathers somewhat so I can
cut or pull out the loose threads with less effort.

When all the stitches have been removed, you'll
be treated not only to the wonderful patterns that
developed within the folds, but also the stitch
tracks. The topography of the fabric is so interest-

The flower stencil design (from The Stencil Co.) was divided into individual sections (flower head, stem, leaves) that could be gathered separately. The leaf shapes were moved slightly away from the flower head for greater design clarity.

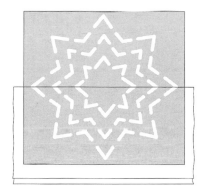

The center line of the stencil is matched to the fold line of the fabric. Only half of the stencil design is traced onto the folded fabric (stencil from The Stencil Co.).

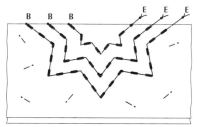

Beginning (B) and ending (E) at the fold line, the traced lines are stitched through both layers of fabric, then gathered and dyed.

TURQUOISE BLOSSOMS quilt by Carolyn A. Dahl. Stitch dyeing, wax block printing, monoprinting, quilting, and turquoise stone beads.

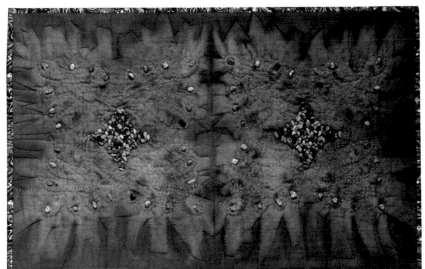

CHAPTER EIGHT

Heat-Transfer Dyes

EVERY SO OFTEN, I find an old embroidery project tucked away in some long forgotten box. The metal hoop has rusted around the dusty fabric making me wonder how old I was when these half-finished flowers were started—eight, nine? What called me away so quickly that I left the still threaded needle dangling?

I remember spending hours in Woolworth's in front of the colorful cubicles of DMC® thread trying to decide which iron-on embroidery pattern I should purchase. I never could decide if my pillowcase needed birds, pansies, a cat, or a puppy with a raised paw. Usually I bought a few of each, as I still do. I guess in the end, it really didn't matter. I seldom finished any of these projects, but I still have stacks of fabric bearing the blue lines of my good intentions.

I didn't know at the time that these iron-on designs awaiting threads were a form of heat-transfer printing. All I knew back then was the magic I still feel—ironing over a piece of paper and finding flowers on my fabric.

FALL MONARCHS by Carolyn A. Dahl. Heat-transferred fabric, black-and-white trans-formed fabric border, embroidered butterfly appliqués from Patch Ems, Rollagraphs® totem masks, screen fade and burlap from Clearsnap, Inc., and flower and stem stamps © All Night Media.

History

The earliest embroidery transfers were composed of printing inks that contained shellac and a colored pigment, usually ultramarine, which gave the characteristic blue-colored lines. More modern forms of heat-transfers evolved when dyers tried to solve the problem of how to color the new man-made fabrics. Up until then, most dyeing processes were for natural fibers, which absorbed dye from a water medium. Man-made fabrics, however, were not absorbent, and new dye classes and methods had to be found.

One of the results of this search was the dispersed (or disperse) dyes developed in 1923, which are used today for most design transfer methods using heat.

Although dispersed dyes solved the problem of how to color man-made fibers, some types of this dye had an annoying characteristic. When the newly dyed fabric was dried with high heat, the dye would vaporize into a gas, float around in the drying chamber, and redeposit on the finished yardage as unwanted specks of color. But as often happens when creative individuals work to correct a problem, the annoyance becomes a new technique.

In 1958, Noel De Plasse discovered that he could make use of this defect by printing patterns with the dye onto paper, laying the paper face down on the fabric, and applying heat to the backside of the paper to vaporize the dye into a gaseous state. Because the vaporized dye was sandwiched between the paper and fabric, it couldn't escape, but would cool and condense onto the fabric according to the design printed on the paper. This new method became known as heat-transfer printing.[1]

It wasn't until about 1968, however, when the first industrial transfer paper was manufactured under the trade name of Sublistatic® that this new process was used to its full commercial capacity. Although most dyers refer to the method as heat-transfer printing, you may find references to it as "sublistatic printing" after the paper's trade name, or "sublimation printing" after its chemical action (turning from a solid, to a gaseous state and back to a solid without liquefying). Whatever it is called, the new technique made it possible to print intricate patterns in rich colors on man-made fabrics. Perhaps some of the best examples of the lavish surfaces this method could produce are the heavily-patterned polyester shirts of the 1970s.

Important Factors

I've included this chapter on the dispersed class of dyes, (heat-transfer dyes) because they offer the ability to reproduce many design possibilities that would be difficult to execute with fiber-reactive dyes directly on the soft, textural surface of cloth (precise lines, detailed stamps, drawings, photographs).

As the most crucial point in using these dyes is the moment of transfer, four materials must interact correctly for your dye to "sublime" and a successful heat-transfer to occur: the transfer paper, the fabric, the heat source, and the dye.

The Paper: In choosing paper to use as the transfer paper, look for one that isn't very absorbent. The fine dye particles should adhere to the paper's surface, but not disappear into its fibers. Many types of smooth, non-textured drawing papers work, as does typing paper for small works. The paper should not be too thick or the iron's heat will not be able to penetrate, nor too thin (if you're painting with the dye), or it will wrinkle from the moisture.

Even the delicate wings of a dragonfly stamp will give a clear image on fabric with the heat-transfer process. Dragonfly stamp © All Night Media.

When stamped images are combined with other techniques such as sponging and marbling, a lot of textural variety can be achieved with only a few images. Composition by Mark Jetton. Stamps: surprised man © Ken Brown Rubber Stamps, lightning © Stamp Oasis, and spark plug © Gumbo Graphics.

2 **The Fabric**: Dispersed dyes were developed for use on man-made fabrics (polyester, acrylic, nylon, or acetate). The greatest permanence and brightest colors are obtained on white, finely woven, 100% polyester fabric. Blends will also give fairly good results, as long as you select one with a high percentage of polyester. One of my favorites is a broadcloth of 65 percent polyester and 35 percent cotton. With this fiber blend, I get good transfer quality because of the high polyester content, but the fabric still has a cotton-like feel. Do not go below a 50/50 blend and don't use 100 percent cotton as the colors will not be permanent.

3 **The Heat Source**: Whatever man-made fabric you use, it must be able to withstand the prolonged heat of a hot iron or commercial heat press. The fabric must not scorch or damage when subjected to the 350 to 400 degree heat of a cotton or hot iron setting. Irons do vary in temperature, however. Test a swatch of your fabric by placing a piece of tissue paper over the surface and iron slowly for approximately 25 to 30 seconds. If the fabric scorches or turns brittle, adjust the iron temperature or select another fabric. The best surface for heat-transfer ironing is a hard, flat one with little or no padding. I use an old, wrinkle-free sheet folded several times over a piece of mat board laid on a hard, heat-resistant surface.

4 **The Dye**: The heat-transfer dye can be purchased in many different forms: stamp pads, wax crayons, marker pens, dye-sheets, and as a dye powder. The color will appear light when it is applied to the transfer paper, but becomes brighter after heated. In whatever form you choose to use the dye, it's best to make a timed test strip of each color to see how it changes after the iron's heat. When the transfer process is completed, the colors are permanent and no further heat setting is necessary. The finished fabric remains soft to the touch and can be dry-cleaned, or gently washed (allow at least 24 hours), and line dried.

FABRIC-TRANSFER INK PADS

A rubber stamp supplier's catalog seems like a scrapbook to me. Images pop off every page and trigger so many personal memories. Looking at a Siamese stamp, I remember my cat Tajma whose gentle love accompanied me through so many studio days. Occasionally, I think I still glimpse her turquoise eyes slipping around a corner.

On another page, the sight of an accordion stamp returns me to being eight years old, holding my little red accordion as my teacher called out in his Swedish accent, *Dragspel Valsen* (Accordion Waltz) or *Varen Polka* (Springtime Polka). Further on, I admire a complex rendering of an armadillo stamp. The first time I saw this strange and wonderful creature was through the glass of my grandmother's china cabinet. Curled up, with its tail in its mouth, the armadillo basket had arrived in Minnesota from my uncle who was in the Army in Texas.

When a stamp draws strong memories out of me, I have to own it and try it on fabric. But memories can be expensive once you are inside a well-stocked stamp store or browsing through a tantalizing catalog. In the beginning, I purchased many stamps that simply would not work on fabric using the traditional fabric colorants. But when I discovered dye-transfer inks, I could once again purchase freely. Almost every image, even the most detailed stamp, can be transferred to a smooth fabric with these inks.

Heat-transfer inks come in pre-inked stamp pads, in twelve ready-to-use colors and are sold under the name Stamp and Press from Center Enterprises. Any rubber stamp can be used with these inks, but it must fit the pad (approximately $3\frac{1}{4}$" x 2") because the inked surface isn't raised so the pad cannot be brought to the stamp for inking. When the stamp is tapped on the pad and pressed to the transfer paper, any images that come out poorly on the paper can be cut away. Other marks such as finger smudges can be painted over with white-out fluid (two coats). Your mistakes are made on the paper, not the fabric.

Because the transfer paper is placed stamped side down on the fabric, and ironed to transfer the images to the cloth, the images will be reversed after transfer.

You can repeat the same stamped image across the paper and iron the whole sheet to fabric for unique mini-yardage for small projects. Or you can create collages for memory books or journal covers by stamping a variety of images that have special meaning for you. Then cut each image out (leave a small border of white paper), arrange them on another sheet of paper, glue the collage in place with glue stick (it doesn't block heat-transfer), and iron the collage to the fabric. The technique allows you to be creative with your stamp collection, make customized birthday or holiday gifts, and experiment with unusual or humorous compositions before ironing them to the cloth.

AND THE CATS JUMPED OVER THE MOON by Carolyn A. Dahl. Mini-quilt made from heat-transfer printed fabric. Rollagraphs® of snakeskin, screen fade, and gravel © Clearsnap Inc.; grapes © Hampton Art Stamps; pear and moon © Rubber Stampede; tic-tac-toe © Inkadinkado; and the Siamese cat © The Stamp Pad Co.

Besides block stamps, Rollagraphs® (rolling wheel stamps with handles from Clearsnap) can be used to create wonderful patterns for backgrounds, borders, or quilt bindings. Rollagraphs print bands of texture (sand, droplets, bubbles, snakeskin) or unique images (holiday lights, totem masks, art angels, exotic birds). The regular size (1" wide) and the jumbo Rollagraph (2" wide), which is perfect for fabric, will print 7¼" of strong color before they must be re-inked. You can push or pull the wheel across the paper carefully matching the stop and start of each band, overprint textures and colors, create curved bands, leave spaces between patterns, or improvise freely.

Select white fabric for very detailed stamp designs so all the fine lines will be visible. When printing block stamps over Rollagraph-patterned backgrounds, use denser, more filled-in stamp designs (see the grapes on page 89).

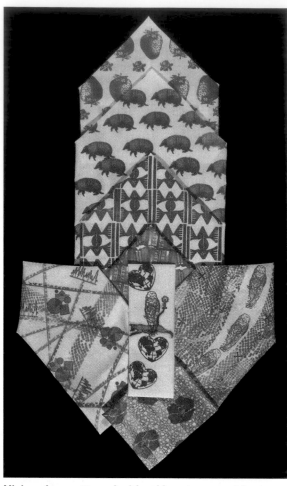

Mini-yardage patterned with rubber stamps and heat-transfer inks. Stamps: strawberry, rose with face, the X, heart-shaped earth © Inkadinkado; armadillo, accordion, Siamese cat, and leopard © The Stamp Pad Co.; frog © Pelle's; candle © Stampendous Inc.; snakeskin and gravel Rollagraphs by Clearsnap, Inc.; icicles, textured geometric shapes, morning glory © Hampton Art Stamps.

Make a beautiful journal or memory book cover with a collage of heat-transferred images. Stamps: Rollagraphs of snakeskin, screen fade and gravel by Clearsnap Inc.; tic-tac-toe grid © Inkadinkado; sand drifts © The Stamp Pad Co.; dragonfly, and rainbow trout © All Night Media, card by Inkadinkado. Fabric by Carolyn A. Dahl and project assembly by Margaret Sindelar.

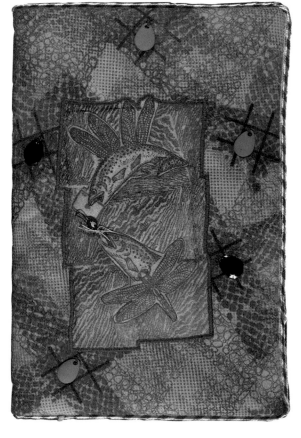

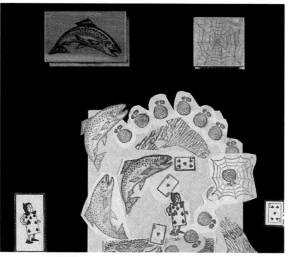

Above: An assortment of stamped images have been cut out and glued to a base paper. Left: The finished heat-transferred collage on fabric. Stamps: rainbow trout, cat face © All Night Media; spider web, oyster, playing card, and card man © Inkadinkado; sand drifts © The Stamp Pad Co.

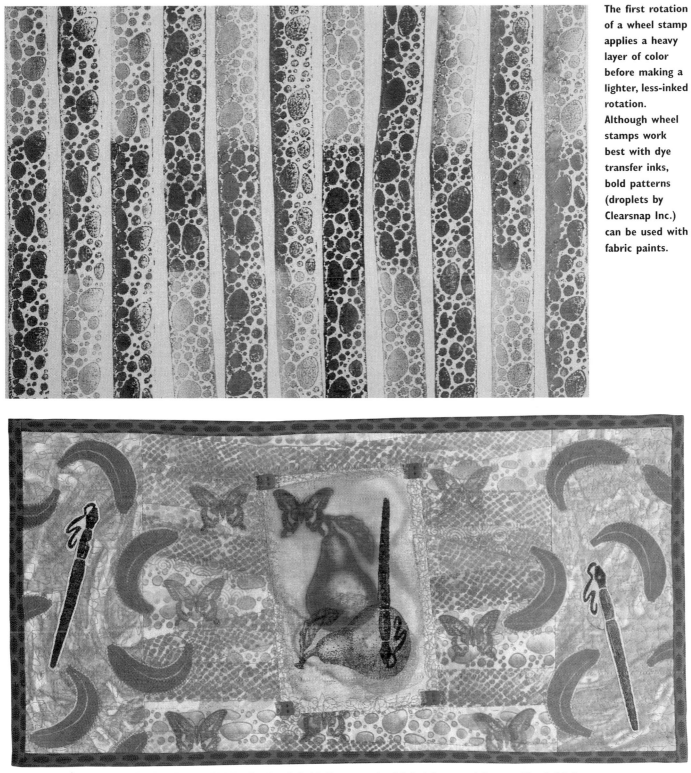

The first rotation of a wheel stamp applies a heavy layer of color before making a lighter, less-inked rotation. Although wheel stamps work best with dye transfer inks, bold patterns (droplets by Clearsnap Inc.) can be used with fabric paints.

BANANAS AND BUTTERFLIES, PENS AND PEARS by Carolyn A. Dahl. Heat-transfer fabric inks on poly/cotton blend, fabric crayon rubbings, quilting and Rollagraphs (snakeskin, droplets, Chinese noodles) from Clearsnap Inc., pear © Rubber Stampede, pen © Posh Impressions, butterfly © The Stamp Pad Co., banana © Hampton Art Stamps.

The heat-transfer process is best used where a small quantity of fabric is needed (although sewing together squares of differently printed pieces can make a large, beautiful quilt). Projects such as miniature quilts, journal and memory book covers, and baby pillows, however, are perfect projects to combine the small images of rubber stamps with the heat-transfer process.

The following demonstration on how to iron-transfer the images from the paper to the cloth is used not only with stamps but with all the other heat-transfer products in this chapter (crayons, pens, dye-sheets, dyes). Because the paper size and dye layer on the paper may differ (stamps leave a thin dye layer on paper that transfers quickly; whereas paint deposits a thicker layer), adjust your heat-transfer time accordingly (consult the manufacturer's instructions).

1 Place typing or computer paper on a smooth piece of scrap paper. Ink the Rollagraph (screen fade) repeatedly by rolling it over the turquoise ink pad until the full circumference of the wheel's surface is evenly coated with ink. Keep the wheel flat on the surface and roll it diagonally across the paper. When the paper is covered with the pattern, wash and dry the stamp and ink it with green ink. Roll it across the paper in the opposite direction.

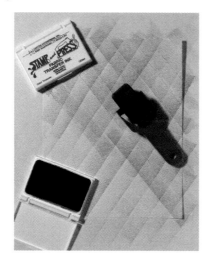

2 Press the fern frond stamp (from Posh Impressions) onto the blue ink pad and stamp the image repeatedly across the paper. Allow the stamped images to dry for 5 to 10 minutes.

3 Heat iron to a cotton or hot setting, or the appropriate temperature for your fabric. Do not use steam. Place fabric right side up on the ironing surface and tape edges. Position the stamped paper, color side down, on the fabric and

cover it with tissue paper. Working in one direction, iron each section of the paper slowly for 10 to 15 seconds or longer. Move the iron slightly as you work to avoid steam hole impressions. To check on the color transfer progress, lift a corner of the paper while keeping the iron in place. (Since odors from heat setting the ink can be unpleasant to some people, wear a respirator and work in a well-ventilated room during this part of the process.)

4 Remove the paper. Your fabric is permanently colored and ready to be used. Projects made from transfer inks can be dry-cleaned or gently washed in cool water (allow 24 hours). It is best to line dry fabric made with transfer inks. And don't throw away your used transfer papers. They can be used to make greeting cards, memory book pages, or journal covers.

FABRIC-TRANSFER CRAYONS & CRAYON CLOTH

Everybody loves a new box of crayons. Although transfer crayons don't come in 100 shades to entice us, Binney and Smith do manufacture eight colors that can be overlaid on the transfer paper for additional color blends to create what I call Crayon Cloth.

Crayola Fabric Crayons work exactly as your childhood crayons, so feel free to scribble on the paper, make rubbings from household objects, draw stick figures like a child, use a page from your favorite coloring book, or transfer your child's drawings to poly/cotton T-shirts.

Unlike the inks used for stamping, crayons deposit a heavy layer of waxy color on the paper. So be sure to check your images for chunks of crayon, which can be removed with the sticky side of masking tape. If left intact, these bits of color could spread into blobs when your design is heat-

Heat-transfer fabric crayons were used on paper (above) and then the finished design was transferred to fabric with heat.

ed. Even worse, they could drop onto your ironing board and suddenly become part of your favorite white blouse.

Wax transfer crayons can also be melted to create designs. Cut or shave the crayon into small slivers and sandwich the pieces between two sheets of paper. Iron over the layers, which will melt the color slivers into the paper and produce two sheets of transfer paper covered in colored spots. All types of the heat-transfer products can be used on the paper together and transferred as one design. So you could add stamped images over the spotted paper before transferring the design to the cloth.

Have fun making Crayon Cloth— scribble, color, outline—rediscover your childhood creativity.

Transfer Pens and Portraits

A sketch portrait of myself at three years old in my favorite dress. The heat-transfer pens work beautifully for line drawings that resemble artist's sketches.

The mad hatter stamp © Inkadinkado was enlarged on the photocopy machine, transferred to the tea cozy shape with Sulky® Iron-On Transfer Pens and enhanced with ZIG® textile markers.

Iron-On Transfer Pens (by Sulky® of America) are the perfect tools for transferring images to fabric when precision is important (line drawings, portraits, words, doll faces). And if you like to work with a pen, you'll love the convenience and flexibility of these special markers, which contain the heat-transfer dye. They come in eight colors and are permanent on the fabric after heat-transfer.

Sketch Portrait

My favorite use for the pens is for portraits, which are often difficult to draw directly on fabric. I've developed three types of portraits that use the heat-transfer pen: the Sketch, the Child Collaboration, and Blind Drawings. When I use the first type, friends often say, "I didn't know you could draw." Well, I can't very well, but I can trace. My secret is to use a photocopy of my subject and trace over the lines, dots, and toner shadings with the Sulky® pens. When transferred to cloth, the technique creates a fairly realistic portrait that resembles an artist's sketch.

A variation of this method is to use the Sulky® Iron-On Transfer Pens to transfer stamp images that have been enlarged on the photocopy machine. For example, I wanted to use some of the images from Inkadinkado's Alice In

The finished tea cozy fabric ready for a mad hatter tea party.

Wonderland stamp set to create a tea cozy. However, I needed larger images than the tiny stamp provided. By enlarging the stamped images on a photocopy machine, I matched the image size to the cozy size. Once the lines of the photocopied images were traced with the Sulky® pens and transferred to fabric, I colored in the images and added pattern with textile markers.

Remember that commercial stamp images are copyrighted. You may use the images for your personal hand-stamping use. However, if you plan to reproduce or enlarge the stamp images for commercial purposes, you must secure the supplier's permission by writing them.

Child Collaboration Portrait

In this portrait style, I provide a stack of paper and encourage a child to make a line drawing portrait of themselves (or someone they know) in one or more transfer pen colors. Then I iron the finished drawings to fabric and complete the collaborative work by embellishing the portrait with regular textile markers. Always make two portraits: one for you and one for the child.

Blind Drawing Portrait

I developed the method of Blind Drawing portraits when I couldn't see well enough to work after eye surgery for a retinal detachment. In order to deal with my fear of losing my eyesight and to keep exercising my creativity, I would close my eyes and begin drawing my face. Often when I

opened my eyes, I'd find the nose, eyes, mouth in the same spot on the paper, but other times, I'd be amazed by the unique portrait my inner mirror provided me.

I've taught this method to many students and am constantly surprised by the resemblance of the drawings to the physical characteristics of the person and her/his emotional state that day. Although I'm able to see well enough to work now, I've never stopped making Blind Drawings because the results are fun, crazy, sometimes scary, but always unique.

My seven year-old nephew Brett Boser and I collaborated on this project. He drew this portrait of me in glasses and I transferred it to fabric with heat-transfer pens.

Procedure

If you'd like to try the technique, place your pencil in the middle of the paper and your other hand on the paper's edge for guidance. Now close your eyes and without lifting your pencil off the paper (or peeking), begin to draw your face. Match your pencil's movement across the paper to your mind as you recite: draw the eyebrow, move down to the top lid of the right eye, the bottom lid, make the circle of the iris, then the pupil, cross over to the center of the paper again, now draw the nose, etc. After you've made many drawings of your face, try adding hands or other favorite objects. Then select your favorite drawings, go over the lines with the Sulky® pens, and iron-transfer the drawings to fabric. Later you can add fabric paint, stitching, beads, or other embellishments.

BLIND DRAWING #3 by Carolyn A. Dahl. Painted cotton, free-style machine stitching, beads, helix sun stamp © Hot Potatoes.

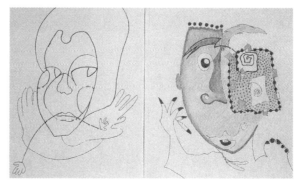

Two examples of my Blind Drawing portrait technique. Colored pencils can be used on the drawings to test different color combinations and stitching ideas.

Dye-Saturated Paper Sheets

BIRTHDAY CARD FOR CANDACE by Carolyn A. Dahl. Dye-sheet photo transfer, MagicStamp® patterned background, birthday buttons.

Iron-Transfer Dyeing Paper (by Carl Manufacturing) sheets are 5" x 7" paper sheets that have been coated with the heat-transfer dyes (dispersed dyes). They can be purchased in thirty colors (color on fabric will be different from color on dyeing paper). Some of my favorites are: Lapis-Lazuli because it resembles old blueprints, Red, Royal Purple, Brown, and Moss Green. Handle the dye-sheets with care so they don't rub against other surfaces and leave unwanted specks of color. Also do not expose the unused paper to strong sunlight.

Although the dyeing paper sheets can be cut into shapes (flowers, geometric, animals) and ironed directly onto the fabric for solid color areas, or used to coat other objects such as dried leaves and flowers for transfer, I prefer to use their rich, evenly-colored surface to transfer photographs to fabric. Of course, if you want a very precise, realistic portrait, you can scan the image on your computer and print it out on the many computer-ready fabrics that are available. However, I like the slightly mysterious, slightly ambiguous quality the dye-sheets give to an image.

One of my favorite uses is to create birthday cloth for someone special. Instead of purchasing a paper card that someone might throw away, I want my birthday wish to continue as long as the cloth lasts. So I fuse a dye-sheet transferred photo of the person onto a dyed or painted background and then add birthday charms or buttons. The project can be as small or as large as you prefer, but I find 5" x 7", 10" x 10", 12" x 12" to be good mailing and framing sizes.

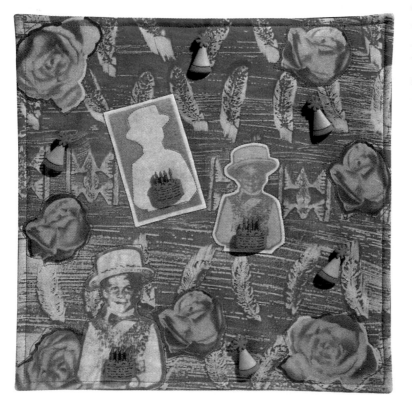

BIRTHDAY PARTY FOR AARON by Carolyn A. Dahl. Dye-sheet photo transfer, painted and stamped background, applique, birthday buttons, feather stamp © All Night Media and frog © Pelle's stamps.

Photograph Transfer with Dyeing Paper

Computer printouts will not work with this process as they have no toner in which the dye can stick. Choose a photograph (black and white works best) that has strong values (definite dark and light areas), a neutral background, and clear sharp details. Copy the photograph on several light and dark settings as each will give different results, as will different machines (the older ones work the best).

Lay the photocopied photograph face down on a dye-sheet. Cover these with tissue paper and iron with a hot dry iron for approximately 20 to 40 seconds, or until the color transfers from the dye-sheet to the photocopy (often the color is subtle). Allow them to cool slightly before pulling apart slowly. Cut away any areas of the background you don't wish to print. You now have a dye-coated photocopy to use as the transfer paper. The used dye-sheet sometimes has a ghost image of the photocopy that can be used also.

Lay the photocopy face down on the cloth. Cover with tissue paper and iron to transfer. If you make a second transfer, which will be lighter, be sure to change the tissue paper which might be contaminated with some of the dye.

POWDERED DISPERSED DYES

Powdered dispersed dyes, called PROsperse dyes, can be purchased from PRO Chemical and Dye so you can mix your own thin (watercolor effects) or thickened colors (painting, screening). The dyes come in fourteen colors, and a starter transfer printing kit is available (contains three colors, plus thickener ingredients, and instructions). Preparing your own colors has many advantages: you can dilute or intensify color values; paint directly on a photocopy; pattern or texturize the paper with sponges, stamps, rollers; save money if you have a large project; hand paint details; and mix your custom colors with all the other heat-transfer products. Another advantage is that you can create dye-sheets of any size. Large photos can be transferred, or flat objects laid on the cloth (leaves, open lace, nets, feathers), a large dye-sheet placed over the objects, and ironed. The objects will block the color resulting in white shapes on a colored background.

If you plan to paint your own dye-sheets for photocopy transfer, use nonabsorbent paper that won't wrinkle from the moisture or you'll get a blotchy transfer. Planned wrinkles can be interesting for some effects though. (See page 66 where I deliberately wrinkled one side of the face transfer.) Apply at least three coats of the dye to the paper for an even coverage, allowing it to dry in between coats. All the images on the photocopy will be reversed when ironed on, so letters and numbers must be painted backwards to print correctly. Let the painted paper dry completely and then follow the same procedure as the Iron-Transfer Dyeing Papers.

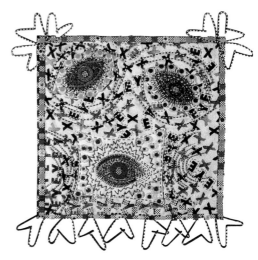

EYE IN EYE #3 by Carolyn A. Dahl. PROsperse dyes used to paint and transfer eye shapes, stitching, wire, plastic eyes. Alphabet stamps © Ranger Industries.

Portrait of my uncle in uniform combines three heat-transfer techniques: a yellow PROsperse dye painted background, Sulky® Iron-On Transfer Pen sketch, and a border of cut dye-paper shapes.

GROWING INTO
MY GRANDMOTH-
ER'S EYES by
Carolyn A. Dahl.
PROsperse dye
photo transfer,
black-and-white
transformed
fabric, grand-
mother's lace
curtains, and
rose embroidery
appliqué from an
old prom dress.

CHAPTER NINE

Hand-Cut Stamps

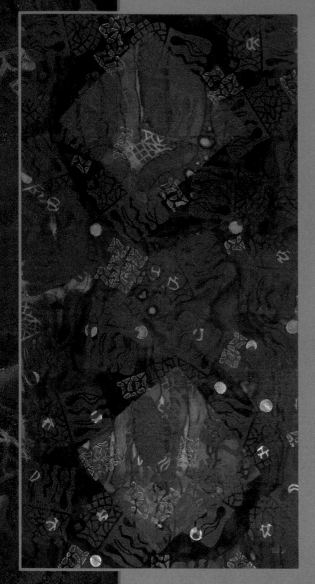

ANY OBJECT CAN BE A STAMP if it can be coated with color and pressed onto fabric. When we made our first "refrigerator art" by dipping our hands into red tempera paint and pressing them to paper, we were using our hands as stamps. A search around the yard, the garage, or through kitchen utensils will quickly turn up other objects that can be used as stamps. However, if you have a specific image in mind, you will want to create your own stamp.

Depending on your design, there are several ways to proceed. If your design has many fine details, and isn't too large, the best choice may be sending your drawing to a commercial company to be made into a rubber stamp for you. If, however, your design calls for bold, simple shapes, it's easy to make your own stamps from sheet or block materials.

Sheet materials are thin (flexible printing plates, sheet foam) and can be cut into shapes and glued to a flat support to create the stamp. Block materials are thicker (erasers, rubber blocks), and are carved to remove the sections of the design you don't want to print. Both materials accept fabric paint or thickened dyes well when applied with a small sponge or brush.

No matter how the stamp is made, the first print will always surprise you. Even though I've planned every detail of the image, spent time carving and building it, I've learned that I don't really know my own stamp until I print it.

ARTFUL CLOTH by Carolyn A. Dahl. Hand-cut eraser stamps, rubber block stamps, and Jacquard metallic paint on hand-dyed silk create a rich visual surface.

Stamp making materials. Starting at left, going down in loosely defined rows.
Row 1: Turquoise sheet foam cut into lace-like design, mounted on foam board, and stamped on fabric with gold paint.
Row 2: Wooden cut-outs; fish stamp cut from flexible printing plate, mounted on foam board and stamped on patterned fabric. Sample at bottom shows a corner of the white protective paper removed to reveal the adhesive-covered gray plate material. Row 3: White rubber block before carving; fabric stamped with a carved figure block; carved eraser stamps and fabric sample; school eraser shapes for stamping. Row 4: Wood carving tools, carved rubber block, and printed fabric.

Detail of ARTFUL CLOTH on opposite page.

DESIGNING YOUR STAMP

Decide if the stamp will be a single unit placed randomly across the fabric, or a unit that touches and interlocks with another to form a repetitive pattern. If used as a random, single unit, any design or image will work. If, however, you want stamp images to form an interactive pattern that changes depending on how the stamp is rotated, you must consider the stamp's outline. For example, if you carved a circle in an eraser, it doesn't matter if you rotate the eraser to the left or to the right, or turn it upside down. The design will always look like one circle next to another circle.

But a stamp with an interesting outline, with edges that protrude and recede, makes new shapes every time it rotates and connects to another.

To test one of your designs, make eight exact squares on a sheet of graph paper. Trace your design onto each square and cut the squares apart. Or you can photocopy your design unit repeatedly, cut out the units, and arrange them into different pattern combinations. Once you have a pattern you like, glue the paper units in place for future reference and begin making your stamp.

Four pattern making possibilities with only two stamp designs.

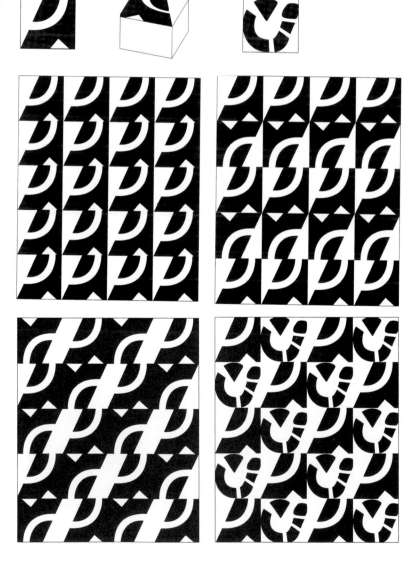

FLEXIBLE PRINTING PLATE

A flexible printing plate is a smooth, durable vinyl-like material, about 1/16" thick, that can be cut with scissors or an X-Acto knife. It is sold in sheets, approximately 9" x 12" and may also be called Sure Stamp or Speedball printing plate. The stamp is made by cutting the image out of the sheet and attaching it with glue stick to a support, such as foam board, cardboard, Plexiglas, or wood. If the support is trimmed to match the contour of the image, about 1/4" to 1/2" from the edge, exact placement on the fabric is easier.

Some brands of the printing plate come with a self-adhesive backing. After tracing your design on the vinyl side (not the paper side) and cutting out the image, the protective paper layer over the adhesive is peeled away and the image is attached easily to the support. If your design is fairly complex, you can attach the printing plate to a cutting surface, cut out the design with a thin X-Acto knife blade, and then reattach it permanently to your support, using glue if necessary.

If you have a problem with the background area printing, you may need to raise the image. Cut an identical shape from the printing plate and attach it onto the one already on your support. The additional layer should give enough depth to keep your background from making contact with the fabric. If not, try stamping on a harder surface.

After stamping, remove the colorant from your design by wiping it with a wet sponge and blotting the stamp repeatedly on paper towels. A soft brush can be used to gently remove color caught in details. Unless your support material is waterproof, do not place the stamp under running water to clean it. Cardboard and paper-covered foam board will deteriorate and warp. A flexible printing plate can also be used to create your own wheel stamps. Cut the pieces of your design out of the plate and glue them to a hard wooden roller.

Flexible printing plate stamp printed on over-dyed, leaf-printed, stamped, and patterned fabric. For dark, dense colors, ink the stamp heavily. Chinese longevity sign stamp © Uptown Design Co.

SHEET FOAM

Usually found in craft stores, these soft foam sheets are fluffier and a little thicker than the flexible printing plates. When selecting sheets, choose those that are free of dents, air bubble holes, and scratches which will print. The foam sheets can also be layered for greater printing depth, and some brands come with a self-adhesive backing. When printed, the image has a slightly granular texture that gives a beautiful quality to bold shapes. Following printing, the foam stamp should be cleaned very gently with a wet sponge to prevent marring the spongy surface.

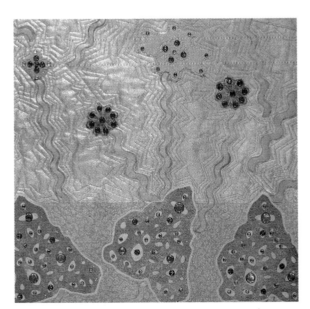

Sheet foam stamps give a slightly grainy quality that adds to the beauty of the print. Detail from FLYING FISH KIMONO QUILT. See page 9 for complete work.

ERASERS

The blue-and-white pattern on this needlepoint canvas was created by eraser stamps, the maple leaf prints by wood cut-out stamps, and the large purple leaves were heliotropic prints.

Eraser stamping is often equated with children's projects and dismissed as too simple to warrant exploration. But complexity of a tool is not important; what is important is the character of the tool's mark. Each material has an individual imprint that cannot be duplicated exactly by another material. If an eraser gives an impression that works with your concept, then it is the right tool to use, simple or not.

I like the humble art gum erasers. They have an uncomplicated, almost primitive charm. Maybe they're not as durable as other erasers, but they are easy to carve and inexpensive. Their surface is small, soft, and tender, forcing me to simplify. When the stamp and I have spent many months together, and its edges get too ragged to print well, I don't abandon it. I simply trim away the bad sections, glue two or three erasers together, and create a new printing block out of their combined images. Finally, when they are beyond hope, I return them to their modest beginnings as functioning art erasers. Within minutes, I've carved a whole new batch of replacements and I'm ready to stamp again.

However, if you want a larger image area, or prefer a harder stamp that lasts for years, consider these erasers: Magicrub, Mars Staedtler Grand, Nasco, Pink Pearl, E. F. Eberhard Faber Plastic Race, RubKleen®, and Pedigree® by Empire.

Carving Erasers

1 Prepare a simple design on paper first. Most erasers have a crumbly consistency and a small carving surface area, so keep the design elements to a minimum.

2 Trace the drawing onto the eraser. Try not to change your mind as the former pencil lines will make indentations in the eraser. Once you ink the surface and press it on the fabric, they will reappear as ghost lines in your design.

3 Using an X-Acto knife, cut away all areas you do not want to print. Insert the knife and cut straight down, or angle away from the design element. Do not undercut.

4 Apply the color with a foam brush or a small cosmetic sponge. Stiff bristled brushes will sometimes scratch the surface of soft erasers. After printing, clean the erasers carefully with your fingers and water. Gentle cleaning is the secret to extending the life of your eraser stamps.

RUBBER BLOCKS

Sold under various names (Soft-Kut, Softoleum, Safety-Kut, Safe N' E-Z Cut, Speedy Stamp Blocks, and Soft Cut), these rubber-like white blocks are the perfect substitute for the hard-to-cut linoleum blocks often used in fabric printing. They can be purchased in small ready-to-carve blocks (4" x 6", 6" x 12" etc.) or in larger sizes (up to 18" x 26"), which can be cut to size. Simply score the surface by pulling a knife along a line, bend the block at that line, and tear the two pieces apart. The depth of most blocks is ¼" or ⅜". The thicker blocks can

be carved on both sides, but I recommend carving only one side as the cuts need to be deeper for fabric printing than for paper printing.

Transferring the Design to the Block

You can draw the design on the block, use tracing paper or Iron-On Transfer Pens by Sulky®, or easiest of all, transfer a photocopy following this procedure.

1 Select a high contrast, black-and-white image or drawing that you want to transfer to the block. Dover books provide some good copyright-free shapes and patterns for generating ideas.

2 Photocopy the image, enlarging or reducing to fit the block. Make copies on several machines as some machines will give good transfers and others won't.

3 Lay the photocopy, image side down, onto your rubber block. Cover both with an old sheet or piece of muslin to act as a pressing cloth.

4 Set your iron to a cotton setting. Press down on the cloth for a count of five with the hot iron. This will cause the toner to stick onto the block so the paper won't shift around as much. Then move the iron in small circles for about 10 seconds or count slowly to 10.

5 Peel back a corner of the photocopy to see if the image has transferred. It should be almost as dark on the block as it was on the paper. If the image looks fuzzy, iron a little longer.

6 When the image has transferred, peel off the paper while it is still warm. The photocopy can often be used two to three times more, so save it. You can now follow the image, which is in reverse, to carve your block.

Photocopies can be transferred to rubber blocks which can then be carved with linoleum cutters or wood carving tools. Erasers are easily cut with X-Acto knives, and sheet foam with scissors.

Carving the Block

My mother had a pet rooster who used to visit the house, sit in her lap, and peck at the door when he was ready to leave. It was a curious choice for a pet to me, so I grew up noticing chickens. Over the years, their images have worked their way into my fabric designs frequently, especially as hand-carved stamps.

The same image, however, can have multiple looks depending on how you carve your rubber block and the choice of background fabric. In the photo below, the stamp block has simple lines and few details, and dominates the dyed background fabric. The same carved block, however, integrates nicely with a textured fabric (printed with a rubber block and thickened dyes) as the colors appear in the white lines. The print almost resembles a woodcut (opposite page). When the same photo copy is transferred again to a new block, but carved with finer tools and more subtle details, the

chicken takes on a more mysterious look (opposite page, lower). Perhaps that's what intrigued my mother. As she once said, "Why would a chicken do that? Leave its own kind and want to live with humans?"

1 Lay the block on a work surface that you don't mind nicking if your cutting tool slips. Covering tables with a piece of strong cardboard or Masonite will help if no other support is available.

2 Carve the design with linoleum cutters or wood carving tools. I prefer to start with a small V-shaped liner tool and outline the design areas I want to keep. Then I switch to a larger U-shaped gouge to remove the background areas I don't want to print. After carving your first block, however, you will know what feels the most comfortable to you.

Whatever method you use, work slowly, carefully, and safely to avoid cutting yourself. Choose

Rubber block stamps printed on wax-patterned and spray-dyed cotton fabric.

Sometimes a
hand-carved
rubber block
almost resem-
bles a wood cut
print.

a quiet, calm time of the day so you can focus and guide the tools smoothly. Coffee addicts like myself should limit their java intake on carving day, as a sure, steady hand is a necessity. To help prevent accidents, always hold the block firmly. The rubbery composition of the material sticks slightly to the work surface, which helps prevent slipping or skidding when carving pressure is applied. However, always keep the non-carving hand well away from the moving tool's path. Wherever possible, work from the interior of the design out to the edge. That way, if you slip, your tool will go off the edge and not into your design, or your hand.

3 After completing the carving, remove all flakes and chunks of rubber that may be caught in the grooves and depressions. Now test your design on a sample piece of fabric. Dab on your color with a sponge or brush and stamp onto fabric. Because the block is thick, you will need to press harder, or rub the backside of the block with your hand, or even pound gently on the block to transfer the color to the fabric. Do not rock or bounce the block, however. Lift the block off the fabric to check the test print. If unwanted background areas have printed, additional carving may be necessary to lower those sections.

4 Clean the block after printing by holding it under water and rubbing the paint off with

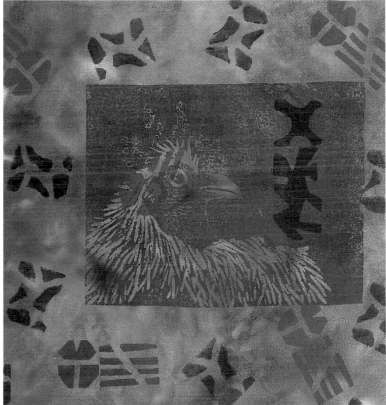

your fingers, or a soft sponge or brush. Soap may be used. Occasionally, after repeated printings with fabric paints, the block continues to feel sticky after washing. Fingernail polish remover can be used to remove some, but not all, paint brands from the rubber surface.

A scrunched, compression-dyed silk fabric (see page 80) provides the perfect background for hand-cut stamp prints.

MAGICSTAMP®

Besides its use in chapter 6, MagicStamp® can also be used to make custom stamps. One method is to press commercial stamps into its heated surface to get reverse images of the stamps. The other is to cover the cold surface of a sheet of MagicStamp® with fabric paint and then draw, scrape, or press textures into the paint. Then the whole sheet is laid on the cloth and pressed as if it were a large stamp. Because the exact pattern isn't repeatable, it's similar to a monoprint process.

MagicStamp® can be used to reverse commercial stamp images and for large, monoprinted designs. Rubber stamp images © Hampton Art Stamps and stencil pattern from Plaid Enterprises Inc.

Shaped rubber block stamps carved by Susan Farm-Heumann.

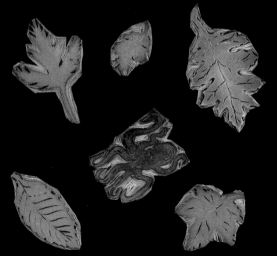

An assortment of rubber block images on fabric by Susan Farm-Heumann.

Susan Farm-Heumann used copyright-free images from a Dover book, "African Designs from Traditional Sources" by Geoffrey Williams, to create her stamps for this vest. Adding a frog shape from Pelle's African image collection, she completed her theme with ethnic-inspired commercial fabric and bone buttons. Versatex fabric paint on cotton.

Destructive Patterns

IF THERE IS A DEMON IN THE MYTHOLOGY OF DYEING, IT WOULD BE BLEACH. A destroyer, it attacks the dye, breaking apart its chemical bonds, and forcing the fabric to release the color. It takes only a few minutes for a rich black fabric to turn brown, then goldish tan, and finally the color of bones.

While bleach destroys the color, it can also be harsh to the fabric. The chemicals that remove the color can seriously weaken the cloth's fibers if careful and correct procedures are not used. Unfortunately, the fiber degradation isn't always apparent immediately.

NUCLEAR FOREST #3 by Carolyn A. Dahl. Silk bleach, multiple dye applications, and slashing were used to achieve the destruction theme I was portraying.

DISCHARGE/BLEACH PATTERNS

I remember a dark gray cotton fabric that I discharged to a dusty pink pattern. I had applied the bleach with a brush in a loose free-form design. As a brush leaves less bleach on the fabric than many other application methods, I wasn't too worried about damage. However, I still checked my fabric for weak areas by holding it up to the light to detect thin spots, and then tugging in both directions on any suspicious looking areas. Thus I was pretty surprised when the second machine washing produced holes in exactly the same shapes as some of the design elements. Apparently, I had made two mistakes. My bleach was too concentrated for the delicate, lightweight cotton, and I had failed to neutralize the fabric properly. The machine's agitation had finally caused the weakened areas to drop entirely out of the fabric.

If bleaching requires such risk, why would anyone want to discharge fabric? Well, maybe you won't. You must be totally entranced and intrigued with the results.

Colors that have been bleached always have an off-beat tonal range. In most fabric design techniques, color is added (or charged) onto the white fabric. But in bleaching, you begin with a commercially- or hand-dyed colored fabric and remove (or discharge, subtract) the color. The color that is left behind always has a peculiar quality. It's not a new color, but one that has disappeared against its will. What remains is like a shadow, or ghost, of a former color.

I've often tried to reproduce a bleached color with my dyes. Although I can come near, my mixture never feels like the color. It never has that disquieting emotional tone. Yes, it's a yellow-green, but it's never the sky-color-before-a-tornado that the bleach leaves behind.

Besides its strange colors, some of the evocative power of discharged fabric comes from the destructive process itself—the fabric's brush with danger. The fabric always carries a trace of the chemical assault in its pattern, and for some purposes and images, I find that a most appropriate characteristic.

When I did my series called the NUCLEAR FOREST silk works, (see also page 112), I wanted to make a statement about destroying the environment. I could think of no textile process other than discharging that would portray a destructive force, and no fabric more precious than silk to represent our beautiful, fragile earth. If I had not been able to chemically attack the silk with bleach, to burn it with fire, and to slash its surface, I would not have been able to convey the statement I wanted to make. Even though the silk works may still look very beautiful in a photo, when the viewer stands next to their seven-foot-high presence, you can feel the assault that took place on their surfaces.

Discharging requires courage. The dyer must risk destroying the cloth to make the fabric become something else. But it also requires diligence. I may let the bleach lead, but I do everything I can to minimize and prevent damage to the fiber. With proper precautions, you can control the demon and produce fabrics with haunting colors and patterns.

Bleach applied to the fabric with a brush gives a dramatic, gestural pattern. Photo by Mike McCormick.

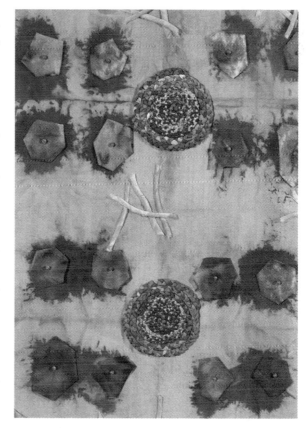

The fabric was hand-dyed a rust color with fiber-reactive dyes. When discharged, the rust turned an interesting light green.

NUCLEAR FOREST
#3 by Carolyn A.
Dahl. Silk bleach,
multiple dye
applications, and
slashing were
used to achieve
the destruction
theme I was
portraying.

MATCH THE FIBER TO THE DISCHARGE AGENT

The discharge agent we will use in this chapter is the familiar chlorine bleach (sodium hypochlorite, or Clorox, Purex). An easy-to-use liquid, chlorine has been around since 1787 when Carl Wilhelm Scheele recognized its color removing properties.[1] It can discharge cotton, viscose rayon, and linen but will damage protein fibers such as silk and wool (consult your dye supplier for the proper bleach for protein fibers).

Not all fabrics can be bleached successfully. Some are too delicate and fragile, have finishes that resist the bleach, or contain dyes that will not discharge (especially expensive fabrics). Although most industrial dyes now in use will discharge to some degree, every so often you will encounter one that refuses to release its color to chlorine bleach. After all, fabric manufacturers spend a great deal of time and money developing colors that won't fade in the wash.

If you're a beginner, avoid very delicate, light-weight fabrics until you have more experience with the process. Start with medium-weight cottons and dark colors which give the most dramatic results. As dark colors are usually composed of mixtures, you never know exactly what color will appear in the bleached areas. Blacks usually yield brown, tan, yellow, or gray-white, but sometimes they'll surprise you with wonderful shades of pink, rust, gold, peach, and even green.

Even though chlorine bleach is a common household laundry bleach, safety precautions are necessary because we are using the product in ways the manufacturer never intended. Usually bleach is diluted with a large amount of water and agitated in a closed machine. With discharge patterning, however, the bleach solution is highly concentrated and hand-applied, which increase your exposure to its corrosive effects.

- Work outside or in a well-ventilated area such as an open garage. Do not inhale the fumes, and always wear a respirator with a multi-gas/vapor cartridge.
- Protect your skin by wearing long-sleeves, long pants, and kitchen (not surgical) rubber gloves. Always protect your precious eyes with chemical splash goggles or safety goggles. Execute all techniques with the fewest splashes or spatters possible.
- Keep bleach out of the reach of children and always cap the container immediately after use.
- Do not mix the bleach with other substances or with other bleaching agents as harmful or irritating gases or vapors could result. Use plastic or glass containers instead of metal.

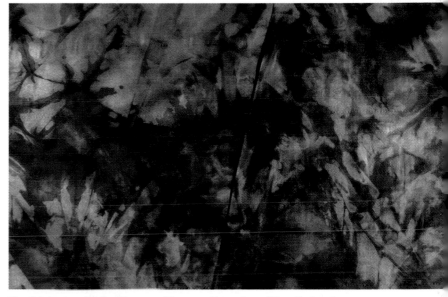

The fabric was dyed with many fiber-reactive colors. After discharging, more dye was added to selected sections. The process was repeated several times with increasingly weaker bleach solutions.

You never know what colors will emerge when black fabric is discharged.

Destructive Patterns 113

Neutralize Discharged Fabric

To stop the chemical action of the bleach, the fabric must be soaked in a neutralizing solution. If you skip the neutralizer and just wash the fabric, you aren't halting the bleaching action immediately. The bleach will become diluted and less powerful in the wash water, but until it is completely removed from the fabric, or neutralized, it will continue acting on the cloth even when dry. We may not need to worry about bleach residue in our laundry as most clothing is replaced within several years, but why jeopardize the longevity of your artwork, when such a simple step prevents damage.

Regular household white vinegar is often used as a neutralizer, but more reliable substances are sodium bisulfite, or Anti-Chlor from Pro Chemical and Dye, or Bleach-Stop (sodium thio-sulfate crystals from Dharma Trading Co., used in fish tanks to remove chlorine from the water). These powders are mixed with water. The fabric is soaked in the solution and rinsed (follow the supplier's specific directions for each product). Once used, however, the neutralizer cannot be reused and must be discarded.

Make Test Samples

Before investing in fabric that may not discharge, purchase 1/8 yard of those colors you are considering and make test samples (following the discharging procedure). Before leaving the store, however, record the label information for each fabric on an index card. You want to be able to find the exact fabric when you return to purchase the cloth. Facing four bolts of black cotton wondering which one gave that subtle salmon color can be most frustrating.

Begin your test by washing the sample fabrics in hot soapy water, rinsing, and drying. Divide each sample piece into six to eight strips. Take one strip and dip a section of it into a plastic or glass bowl containing a 50 percent bleach to 50 percent water solution. I start my testing with this ratio, but often find the solution isn't strong enough to discharge many of my samples. But seeing as the goal is to use the least amount of bleach to achieve the discharging, I start with this concentration and add bleach as necessary.

Keep careful notes on each index card as to how long the fabric took to discharge, the bleach concentration, and the colors that evolved as the bleach progressed. When the strip reaches a color you like, immediately place it in the neutralizer to stop the action.

If the fabric color didn't change at all on some of your strips, mix up a stronger solution, take a new strip of that color, and try again. Continue adding small increments of bleach to the solution until you get the results you want. If the fabric simply doesn't change color at all, eliminate it from your choices. After neutralizing, washing, and drying the samples, attach them to your index cards for future reference. Once you've identified the fabrics that will discharge, you can return to the fabric store and purchase the amount needed for your project.

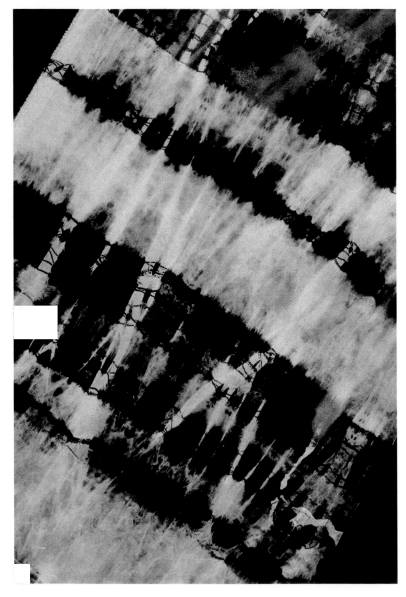

Binding the fabric with string and applying the bleach in bands creates fold-like shadows within the stripes.

Discharging Procedure

Almost any technique in this book can be used to create a discharge pattern if you substitute bleach for the coloring agent. Try binding, stamping, painting, leaf printing, folding and dipping the edges, and pouring the bleach over objects. If your patterning process is slow, such as printing with bleach, the areas discharged first will have a longer time to react producing lighter colors than those done more recently. So start with fairly short lengths of fabric.

Sodium alginate or monagum (a starch) can be added to thicken the bleach solution for stamping and printing procedures. The thickened paste will last only two to three hours, however, as the bleach breaks down the binders rather quickly. So mix up only as much discharge paste as you can use in one session. A synthetic thickener (called Bleach Thickener from Dharma Trading Co.), however, will last for approximately 24 hours. Another useful product is the ready-to-use Discharge Paste from Jacquard. You apply the bleach paste to the fabric, let it dry, and then iron the fabric with a steam iron to remove the color (do this outside wearing a respirator and eye goggles).

Sometimes the weather affects the speed of the bleaching action. Cold slows the bleach's action. But if you're working in full sun on a hot day, the bleach will work faster. I recommend that you set up a process assembly line (safety gear, the bleach solution and tools you'll need, first bucket of rinse water, second rinse bucket, neutralizer bucket, and third rinse bucket). You don't want to be mixing the neutralizer as the wonderful coral color you loved turns into a tan.

When your fabric changes to the color you've been waiting for, immediately plunge it into the first bucket of rinse water to remove excess bleach, then quickly swish it in the second rinse, and then into the neutralizer. Agitate the cloth for about five minutes. Most fabrics can remain in the neutralizer without damage (no more than 20 to 30 minutes), giving you time to discharge the next piece of cloth. I usually work within color groupings as some of the discharging color bleeds into the neutralizing solution and could redeposit.

Remove the fabric from the neutralizer, and place it in the last bucket of rinse water to remove the neutralizer. Then machine wash and dry the fabric. To prevent any damage to the brushes or implements I used during the bleaching process, I also give them a dip into the neutralizer, followed by a thorough water rinse to be sure all chemicals have been removed.

After discharging your fabric, you can over-dye the fabric, paint new colors into the discharged areas, use the fabric as a base for stitching or beading, or store your fabric for future use.

Wooden printing blocks dipped in bleach (or painted with discharge paste) offer a variety of images, textures, and patterns on embroidered black cloth.

After you've discharged black cloth, why not experiment with a variety of other colors? You can dye your own fabric or purchase richly-colored commercial fabric. This project features spraying bleach through a plastic chili stencil (or select your own design) onto red cotton. Once the discharging is finished, you can embellish the design with stitching and beads, paint into the discharged areas, or use the same stencil to add gold accents on the chilies. It's a fun project to create a Christmas hanging, Valentine Day pillows, or place mats to perk up your kitchen.

Supplies
- String of Chilies stencil by Delta
- 1 yd. red fabric, 100% cotton
- Newsprint or newspaper
- Rocks (or weights)
- Chlorine bleach
- Small spray bottle
- Neutralizer
- 4 Plastic buckets or pans
- Safety gear

1 Lay fabric on a surface that won't be damaged by bleach. Position stencil on the right side of the fabric.

2 Cover remainder of fabric with paper to protect it from the spray. Weight with rocks. Wearing safety gear, lightly spray bleach over stencil.

3 Remove paper. Move stencil to the center of the fabric. Hint: watch for drips from the wet stencil.

4 Cover remainder of fabric with newsprint, but leave a band of fabric exposed above and below the stencil. Weight paper and spray bleach over the stencil.

5 Remove paper on the left only and move stencil to the left.

6 Cover everything except the stencil with paper, weight it, and spray bleach over stencil openings.

7 Remove paper and stencil, soak the fabric in the neutralizer, machine wash and dry.

DEVORÉ OR BURN-OUT TECHNIQUE

In discharged patterns, our goal was to control the destruction of color without harming the fiber. In the devoré technique, however, our aim is to destroy and remove the fiber. Devoré is a French word for devour or destroy, but I think of it as fire in a bottle. One puts the gel paste on the fabric, applies heat, and the fiber is quickly reduced to ash-like fragments.

But, this is not true for all fabrics. The devoré gel is particular and removes only cellulose fibers such as cotton, viscose rayon, ramie, and linen. Synthetic fibers (polyester, nylon, and metallic) and protein fibers (silk and wool) are safe from its burning fire. Immediately we can see how this unique characteristic has potential for making patterns on fabric. You can choose a cellulose fabric if a totally burned out area is wanted, or a mixed content fabric if only half of the fiber is to be removed (the cellulose threads) and the other half left intact (the synthetic or protein) for a cutaway effect.

The ingredient that removes the cellulose fibers is sodium bisulfate, or as it is often called in Europe, sodium hydrogen sulfate. This highly acidic ingredient (pH-1) is added to a thickener to create a gel paste. You can purchase the gel ready-to-use as Fiber-Etch® fiber remover from Silkpaint Corporation (there's also a Paper-Etch dissolving gel for paper and wood). I prefer to use this premixed paste as it comes in a convenient squeeze bottle with a good drawing tip, and I don't have to store the chemicals. However, if you plan to use the paste in a large quantity, you may want to mix your own. The recipe and industrial gum thickener needed to make the gel paste are available from Silkpaint Corporation. The sodium bisulfate can also be purchased from a pool supply store as a pH decreaser for spas and hot tubs. The one I use is Bio Guard, SPA Guard. Others are available, but check the label to be sure they contain sodium bisulfate.

Uses of the Devoré Technique

Devoré can be used to remove areas enclosed by a resist (fabric paint, iron-on appliqués, wax, or machine embroidery) for cutwork patterns without any frayed edges. Its ability to remove fabric from areas too tiny for scissors makes it useful for buttonholes also.

When using fabric paint, the paint must penetrate to the backside of the fabric. Allow the paint to dry completely and then apply the paste next to the paint lines. Dry the devoré paste promptly with a hair dryer. As ironing to activate the devoré paste might flatten the paint line, a heat gun directed at the backside of the fabric can be substituted (beware of scorching). Be sure that your paint can be subjected to high heat safely.

If stitching is used as a barrier, your thread should be 100 percent polyester, nylon, silk, or metallic so it won't be devoured by the paste. Metallic thread should have a polyester, not a rayon, core. Most of the flat tinsel threads are polyester and metallic.

According to the Silkpaint experts, a design should be satin stitched onto the fabric using a stitch length of .35 mm to .50 mm. Then stitch a width of at least $1/16$" so that the paste will stay within the enclosed area. They also warn that some blue, or blue-toned, acrylic thread dyes change color when touched by the devoré paste. So, always test your thread first. When ironing to activate the paste, metallic and acrylic threads may need a lower temperature for a longer time because of their content.

Quilted pieces with satin-stitched design areas can also be burned out if cotton quilt batting and cotton fabrics are used. As the quilted sandwich will be thick, you need to apply the gel paste to both the front and back of the satin-stitched design areas. The paste will eat through one layer at a time and not destroy the stitched areas if the proper thread is used.

2 It is also used to burn out shaped holes in cellulose fabric by drawing onto the fabric with the paste without any resist barriers. The end result will be intentionally frayed, ragged shapes creating a distressed look.

On the vest, Iris Lee stitched the design through two layers of cellulose fabric, and then used Fiber-Etch® in the stitch enclosed areas to burn out both layers. In the background fabric, I drew with Fiber-Etch® on 100 percent cotton fabric. Without any resist (stitching, paint) to block the solution, I got the frayed X pattern I wanted.

3 Devoré will create transparent and opaque areas on one piece of mixed fiber cloth. This works especially well on lightweight white fabric to achieve a subtle contrast of whites, and on rayon/cotton velvets for a textural contrast.

4 It also has the ability to change the structural strength of the cloth. Removing all or some of the woven fibers in areas causes those sections to collapse, or become less firm.

5 Finally, devoré can be used to make clean-edged reverse appliqué without using scissors. If two different fabrics are satin stitched together (for example, cotton on top and polyester on the bottom) and the devoré gel paste is applied to the top cotton layer, the cotton will disappear and reveal the polyester fabric underneath.

Fabric Selection

As in discharging, purchase a small amount of fabric and test it at home first. How a cloth is woven (which fiber is the weft and which is the warp) can be very important to the final effect, especially in blends. Avoid selecting fabrics with surface finishes or patterns that have been printed heavily with pigments. With fiber blends, I find that the cellulose content needs to be at least 50 percent to get clean burnout patterns.

Your best chance of success is to use those fabrics recommended for devoré by the fabric suppliers listed in this book. Silkpaint Corporation sells a 55" wide, white, 50 percent poly-cotton blend called azeta that I like especially. This batiste-weight fabric from England becomes very translucent in the burned-out areas. Other good combinations are 50/50 silk/linen, silk/cotton, wool/rayon, cotton/polyester, and silk/rayon velvet often seen in scarves.

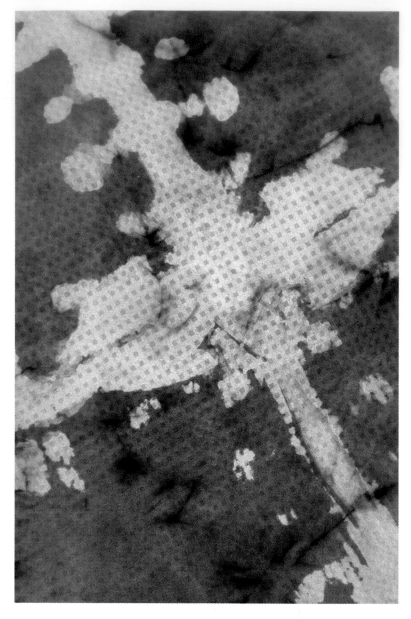

Commercial fabric, woven in an open-work pattern, will complement your hand-devoréd pieces in projects where large quantities of fabric are needed. This cloth was dyed pink with fiber-reactive dyes, folded into a bundle, and only its edges dipped into the bleach.

Burn-Out Procedure

When working with the devoré paste, mixing your own, or heat activating the gel paste, be sure to wear protective gear (gloves, respirator, eye goggles). The ingredients can be irritating to the eyes, skin, nose, and throat.

1 Secure your fabric to newspapers with tape or pins, or stretch it in an embroidery hoop. Shake the plastic squeeze bottle, or stir the devoré gel paste well. Apply the paste in a thin layer (not raised) from the tapered spout or paint it onto the right side of the fabric. Allow to air dry. A hair dryer can be used to dry small or detailed areas, but large areas will take some time to dry (avoid leaving the paste on the fabric overnight as it may degrade the fibers). If you unintentionally spot the fabric, apply baking soda to the still damp area or wash with soap and water before it dries.

Besides applying the gel paste by hand, an Air Pen™ from Silkpaint can be used. It works like a fat pen connected to an electric air pump and disperses a continuous flow of the devoré paste. Other mediums such as fabric paint, resists, and thickened dyes can also be run through the pen for long and flowing lines.

2 Protect your ironing surface with paper. Unpin the fabric from the newspaper or hoop, lay it face down on the surface, and cover with a piece of thin fabric or tissue paper to protect your iron. Although the paste won't stick to the iron, it can discolor the metal. The falling-out fibers can also collect in the steam holes. Begin to iron the fabric on the reverse side. Use a wool setting or a temperature appropriate to your fabric and iron. Do not use steam. I always do this procedure outside to ensure adequate ventilation (a heat gun can also be used carefully and velvet can be heated in a tumble dryer).

3 When the pasted areas have turned a cafe-au-lait color (light brown), the chemical action is complete. Do not overheat or over-iron the fabric. The pasted areas will feel brittle to the touch when sufficient heat has been applied.

4 Place the fabric under a gently running faucet to rinse away the fiber fragments from the pasted areas. You may need to lightly rub with your finger to remove all the burned out fibers and residual paste.

If you are using a blend fabric but find that both the cellulose and other fibers have been removed, try the process again. This time, use less devoré gel paste and less heat. The devoré technique is an industrial method done under very controlled conditions. Sometimes, we need to experiment several times with the same fabric to discover the exact amount of paste, the correct temperature setting time with our equipment, and the right color tone of the burned-out areas to achieve the same success as a commercial producer.

Rayon velvet dyed with fiber-reactive dyes. See chapter 2.

CHAPTER ELEVEN

Wax Patterns

BATIK IS THE FIRST WORD THAT COMES TO MOST MINDS WHEN A HOT WAX TECHNIQUE IS MENTIONED. Inspired by the exquisite beauty of Indonesian fabrics, many of us embarked on insanely ambitious batik projects. After days of dyeing and waxing, we ended up with permanently colored bathtubs and a closet full of board-like fabrics that never would release all their wax.

Yet, I have wonderful memories. I think of the process as a "grandmother technique" as it taught me so much about dyeing, the labor required, and respect for the craft. Whenever I come across a scrap from the fifteen yards of batiked curtains that clogged my bathtub drains with solidified wax, I still smile. I think everyone should try batik, at least once for the memories, and to develop a real appreciation for the simpler technique of dye painting with wax resist lines.

The white wax lines give a bold, stained-glass look to any design. Photo by Mike McCormick.

DYE PAINTING WITH WAX RESIST

In batik you save color areas by covering them in hot wax before submerging the fabric in a dye bath. Although the saved colors remain bright, the background can turn muddy after about four to five dye baths. It's extremely difficult to achieve color variety when one color is constantly dyed on top of another. But in dye painting, the area you want to dye is outlined, not covered with wax, and the color painted into or around the shape, much like a stained glass window. As the fabric is never immersed, you can add as many colors as you desire, in any sequence, and still have a brilliantly-colored final product. You must like the look of a drawing, however, as the lines surrounding each shape will always be an integral part of the final design.

Because the dye is painted into wax-enclosed spaces, you can use many different colors on one piece of fabric.

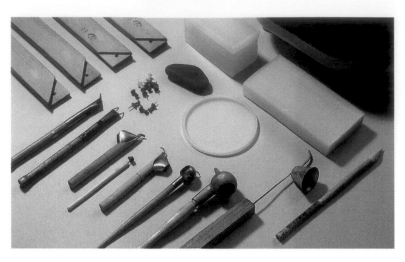

Tools needed for the process: Tjanting tools for hot wax drawing, interlocking wood bars and push pins for stretching fabric, rock for tjanting rest, plastic lid for drips, paraffin and beeswax, electric fry pan with thermostatic control, and a wax brush.

Process Overview

To create a design, hot wax is used as a resist and applied to the fabric with a tjanting tool. Similar to a thick pencil, it has a metal cup at one end to hold the hot wax, one or several spouts through which the wax flows, and a wooden or bamboo handle. The spout openings may be tiny, as in the Pyssanka tool for Ukrainian batik eggs, or large enough to cover sections of the fabric. Think of it as a pen for writing, except the ink is hot wax. Tjanting tools may be manual or electric, with different size spout openings (small, medium, large, and extra large), depending on the width of the line to be drawn. Some have multiple spouts, up to seven, for drawing those perfect parallel lines we see in Indonesian batiks.

Wherever the wax line is drawn, the color of the fabric is preserved underneath as the dye cannot penetrate the wax barrier, nor spread beyond the outline. Liquid fiber-reactive dyes are brushed into the unwaxed areas while the fabric is horizontal, stretched over a wood frame or suspended on harite (see page 130). Once dry, the fabric is heat-set to make the dyes permanent, and the wax is removed. If your original fabric was white, all your painted shapes will be outlined in white. If the fabric was multicolored, the lines will be multicolored after wax removal. Excess dye is then washed out and the fabric is ready to use.

Selecting the Wax

Although we tend to think of natural beeswax when we hear the word wax, many synthetic waxes, or combination mixtures are available. In some cultures such as Indonesia, the wax resist recipes are kept secret. For although they may contain the basic beeswax and paraffin, many other ingredients such as gums and resins are added to suit the working methods of the individual artist.

Paraffin Wax

This petroleum-based, inexpensive wax can be found in supermarket canning sections (or from dye suppliers) and comes in block form (1- to 10-lb. sizes), or as granules for use in electric tjanting tools. It is the best wax to use for the traditional batik crackle effects as it has little flexibility. Melting point is 135 to 140 degrees Fahrenheit.

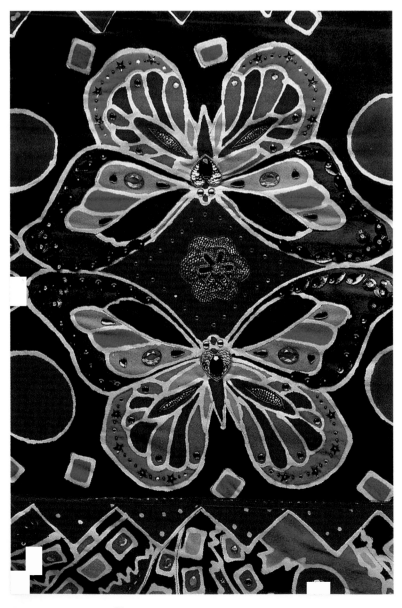

Detail of the back of METAMORPHOSIS COAT. Photo by Mike McCormick.

Beeswax

The natural product of the Apis mellifera (honey making bee), which secretes flakes from its wax glands to build combs for its young and to store honey. Wax purchased from dye suppliers has been processed to remove all impurities and moisture left in the wax. Usually beeswax is blended with paraffin to reduce costs and because it is more flexible and doesn't crack or flake off the fabric as easily as pure paraffin. Working with beeswax is pleasant as it has a lingering fragrance reminiscent of its flower source and a beautiful creamy color. If you do your waxing outside near flowers, you may have a few bee visitors who seem to be drawn to their own beautiful product. Melting point is 130 degrees Fahrenheit.

Microcrystalline Wax

A synthetic wax often substituted for beeswax (and also called "sticky wax"), it is a petroleum-based product that can be added to paraffin instead of the more expensive beeswax. Microcrystalline wax comes in one-pound blocks and has a melting point of 160 to 170 degrees Fahrenheit.

Batik Wax

Usually a blend of 25 percent microcrystalline wax with 75 percent paraffin, it is sold premixed in granulated form. Easy to melt, it's perfect for electric tjantings. Melting point is 150 degrees Fahrenheit.

Wax Safety

I use a mixture of half paraffin and half beeswax. The wax can be melted in a double boiler, but an electric frying pan with a thermostatic control is safer as it keeps the wax a constant temperature. I set the dial to 160 to 225 degrees Fahrenheit, depending on the fabric thickness. A thick fabric requires a higher temperature to penetrate the

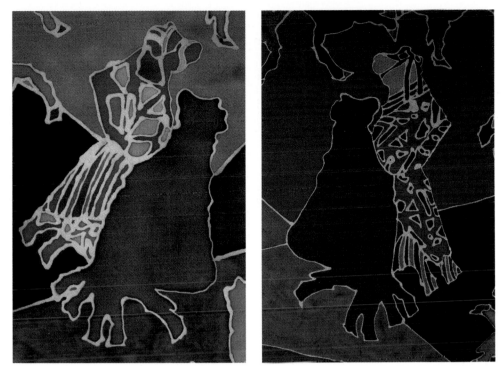

dense fibers (such as cotton velvet); whereas a thin silk would need a lower temperature to control wax spreading.

Always work in a well-ventilated room, or place the pan under a kitchen stove's exhaust fan (protect your stove from drips), or better yet, work in an open garage or outside as I do. If you have any allergies to wax fumes or respiratory sensitivities and are working with a light- to medium-weight fabric, you may want to substitute water soluble resists or gutta serti for the wax (see page 142).

Never leave the wax unattended! If the phone rings, or if you are finished for the day, shut off the pan and pull out the plug. Most of us tend to think of wax as a harmless substance found in crayons, food, cosmetics, and candles. But like fat in a frying pan, it is combustible and can cause a fire. If it begins to smoke, turn down the temperature immediately. Keep a box of baking soda and the pan's lid nearby to smother flames should they ever occur. Never place a pot of wax directly on an open flame and keep it away from children and pets.

Handled properly and watched closely, wax is not dangerous and shouldn't scare you. The key is knowing the risks and then following procedures that eliminate them.

Once the basic shapes are outlined in wax, you can improvise patterns within each shape. Detail of dancing cow couples from CAROLYN'S COWS BREAK LOOSE AT THE DANCE by Carolyn A. Dahl.

PLANNING THE DESIGN

You can either draw with your tjanting directly onto the fabric, or draw your design on paper first and transfer the design to the fabric. For beginners, I recommend drawing directly on the fabric by making a sampler that will later make a beautiful pillow cover. Cut the fabric to fit the dimensions of four wood stretcher bars assembled to make a frame. For example: If you cut a 19" fabric square to fit a 19" frame, the inner dimensions of the frame—your painting area—will be approximately 16" which is perfect for a pillow. With the fabric on a smooth, wax paper-covered surface, draw four squares (or more) that connect. Within these squares, draw lines, circles, dots, flowers, or any pattern that you like. If you want an enclosed shape, each line must connect with another or the dye will escape.

The other method is to preplan your design on paper first. Inexpensive drawing paper, roll paper, or the dull side of butcher paper may be used (avoid glossy paper, except for wax paper). Until you've had some experience with the wax and tjanting tool, avoid drawing very close lines or detailed shapes as the wax spreads on the fabric. Whether the design is simple or complex, it should be the same size as the finished work. For instance, in my silk work series called OUTER SPACE, each hanging is 80" long and 45" wide so my drawings had to be the same size.

When the drawing is complete, trace the lines with a black permanent marker and tape it to a smooth, protected surface. Lay the fabric over the drawing; the black lines should be visible through the fabric. Secure the fabric with masking tape to prevent shifting. Then trace the drawing's lines with the tjanting and hot wax (see page 145).

An alternative method is to wax the fabric after it has been stretched on the frame instead of when it is lying flat on a surface. The drawing is pinned to the underside of the fabric and removed after waxing. Some artists prefer this method because it reduces the possibility of damaging a waxed line while stretching. Try both methods and decide which works best for you and your design. For instance, if I am doing a very precise, detailed image, I find I have more control over the tjanting tool if I can rest my arm on a hard surface, instead of working over a frame edge on a suspended fabric.

If the fabric is too dense to see your paper design, you can draw directly on the fabric with a soft charcoal stick or an Ebony pencil. Tracing over the drawing with Sulky® Iron-On Transfer Pens and ironing the design onto the fabric also works. The Sulky® pen lines, however, will become permanent, so you need to incorporate them into your overall design. Disappearing transfer ink pens may also be used, but should be tested first as some inks become permanent on contact with hot wax or dye chemicals.

OUTER SPACE silk work series by Carolyn A. Dahl. Gallery installation.

USING THE TJANTING TOOL

Batik may very well owe its name to the mark of the tjanting tool.[1] The characteristic use of the tjanting tool in the designing of Indonesian fabrics is to outline a pattern in tiny drops of wax. Tik refers to a little bit, or a drop, thus a fabric called batik has in its name the process by which it was made. Batik can also mean wax writing[2] and as the tjanting is often called a wax pen, the tool's mark and the batiked cloth do seem linked in origin.

The word *tjanting* is a visually interesting word. Unfortunately, the Indonesian government has modernized its language and officially changed tjanting to canting tool. I, however, plan to continue using the old, more exotic spelling. When a word seems to fit the personality and cultural history of the tool, I hate to let it disappear from the dyer's vocabulary.

Even though the name may be old-fashioned, the tool need not be. Today one can choose to use the traditional, manual tjanting tool, or the modern, electric version. If you don't mind always being connected to a cord, the electric tjanting has several advantages. The wax flakes or granules are fed directly into the heated reservoir, so you do not need to tend a wax pot and fumes are minimal. The wax in the reservoir is kept at a constant temperature because of a built-in thermostat so the wax flow is more steady than in a hand-dipped tjanting. Although the time may vary, most manufacturers claim that one filling will last from 5 to 10 minutes, which means that longer lines can be drawn with fewer breaks.

With a manual tjanting, the waxer must control more variables. Working with the tool can be a beautiful process, but it does require some practice and concentration because it is a more primitive tool. The control is in the hand, not technology.

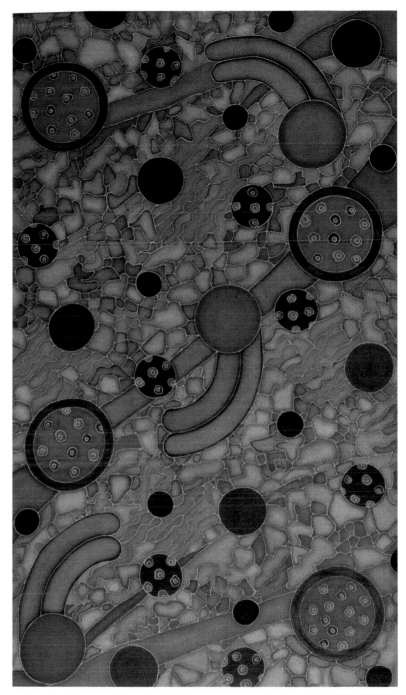

GALAXIE STORM by Carolyn A. Dahl. Dye painting with wax resist on silk habotai. Part of OUTER SPACE silk work series.

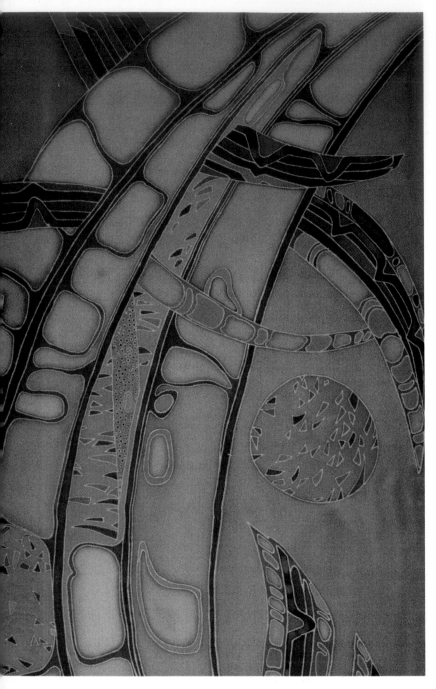

MOON SLIVER by Carolyn A. Dahl. Dye painting with wax resist on silk habotai. Part of OUTER SPACE silk work series.

drips. Move the tjanting to the starting point on the fabric and remove the lid to release the flow of wax.

Work quickly and skim over the fabric, making sure that all lines connect. Do not press the tip hard against the fabric or the wax will stop flowing. It helps if you work from left to right to assure that any wrinkles produced will be released at the fabric's edge. When the tjanting needs to be refilled, replace the lid under the spout as you move over the fabric back to the wax pan.

Look closely at the waxed lines on your fabric. If the wax has penetrated the fibers, it will look translucent and smooth. If it has a milky, rough, opaque look, the wax needs to be hotter to penetrate completely. Also remember to watch for breaks in the lines where dye might escape into unwanted areas. To correct a break, wax over the exact spot on the fabric, or touch up with a fine wax brush.

Don't be discouraged if at first your lines are wobbly and the tjanting tool feels awkward. With time you will understand its ways. Sometimes two or three tjantings must be tried to find the one that seems to match your hand.

Wax lines reflect your mood like handwriting. It's not a process you do when you are agitated or distracted. In fact, Indonesian women used to meditate to reach the proper state in which to begin work[3] because they knew how responsive the tjanting was to one's temperament. Good work was only possible "on a good day with tools that were blessed."[4] In a book by F. Anderson, craftsman Aisjah Soedarsono sums up the connection between one's spirit and the work with these words: "We batik both sides. It's part of the old Javanese philosophy that holds that a person should be the same inside and out. In other words, be honest to himself ... During the time you work on batik, you shouldn't talk. Your feelings should be quiet and clear."[5]

Submerge the manual tjanting's spout into the hot wax (rest it against a rock placed in the wax pan) to heat the metal reservoir and to fill it ¾ full. When you lift it out of the wax, place a plastic lid (or folded towel) under the spout to catch

STRETCHING THE FABRIC

If you waxed your fabric on a flat surface, remove the tape and gently separate the waxed fabric from the wax paper or your drawing. Work slowly to avoid cracking the wax lines. Lay the fabric over canvas stretcher bars (available in art supply stores) assembled into a frame. Attach the fabric with push pins while stretching it slightly. There should be no low spots and the fabric should spring back to the touch. The fabric will sag when wet, so elevate your frame with plastic cups (bricks, cat food cans) so it won't touch your work surface.

If the fabric is too long for stretcher bars, you will want to stretch the fabric like a hammock. The Japanese use *harite* (also known as *hariki*), which are wooden fabric grabbers, or clamps, that run the full width of each end of the fabric. Think of them as jaws (two boards hinged together) that bite down on the fabric with metal teeth (small nails that fit into holes) to hold the fabric while it is being stretched lengthwise (the warp) between two supports. As harite are easy to make yourself, I have many sets that match the various widths of the fabrics I use. However, if you plan to purchase only one set, get the widest size (60") which will accommodate all fabric widths (available from John Marshall; see Supply Sources).

Even after the fabric is stretched lengthwise on the harite, it will still have some ripples running from selvage to selvage. Thus *shinshi*, which are bamboo sticks with sharp needle-like metal points in each end, are inserted in the fabric selvages across the width (woof) at intervals. Because the shinshi length is slightly greater than the fabric length (approximately 2" to 2½" longer), the flexible bamboo bends, causing enough tension in the fabric to straighten out the ripples.

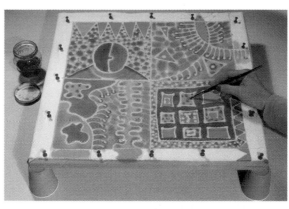

After waxing the design, the fabric is stretched on a frame, elevated, and painted with fiber-reactive dyes.

The waxed fabric for the METAMORPHOSIS COAT (see page 133) was suspended like a hammock with harite and shinshi to keep it taut for painting. Working on all the pattern pieces at the same time helps to visualize color placement throughout the garment. Photo by Dan Sharp.

1 Purchase four pieces of unfinished wood, either ¾" x ½" or 2" x ½". Cut each piece 8" to 10" longer than your fabric width. You will need two boards per set.

2 Mark the top board of each set with the following measurements:
For cord holes: 1" to 1½" in from each end
For nail holes: ½" to 1" intervals across length

3 Lay each marked board on top of an unmarked board and clamp ends together with C clamps. Hammer thin, sharp nails into the top board following the nail hole marks. The nails should be long enough to go completely through the top board and into the bottom board about ¼" to ⅜". Drill the cord holes completely through both boards.

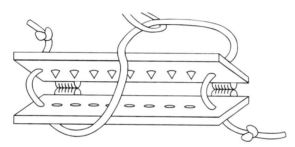

Harite with traditional cord tie-up.

Author's cord tie-up so harite can be moved to a vertical position for viewing fabric.

4 Remove the clamps and pry the two boards apart. The top board will have nails protruding from it and the bottom board will have matching holes. If you have difficulty with this system, you can do the boards separately. Pound the nails through the top board, press them into the bottom board to make nail indentations, and then drill out the nail holes and cord holes separately.

5 Add two or three hinges to one side of the set to connect the two boards and make the "jaw." Run a strong cord or rope through the cord holes. The traditional method is to thread one end of the cord through the top of one side and the bottom of the other. This method helps keep the clamps from popping open. I, however, like to look at my work in a vertical position. So I avoid the knots, and run the cord under the bottom board so I can slide the harite in any direction I choose. To keep the harite closed, I use masking tape or loop the cord around each end.

6 Center the fabric over the nails (the teeth). Attach one end of the fabric to a nail point, stretch it slightly over the other points, and attach to the last nail it reaches. Close the harite and the teeth will penetrate the fabric.

7 Connect your cord to another cord that will attach to a hook, post, or hammock stand for slinging the fabric. If the second cord has a slip knot you can adjust your fabric's tautness as you work.

8 Insert the shinshi across the width of the fabric (selvage to selvage), and you're ready to paint.

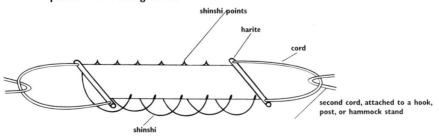

Fabric stretched between poles with harite and shinshi.

PAINTING THE FABRIC

This is the exciting part. Load an inexpensive watercolor brush (dye chemicals can ruin expensive brushes) or a foam rubber applicator with activated fiber-reactive dyes (use the H series if the design will take several days to paint). Touch the brush to the center of a wax enclosed space and watch the dye spread until it bumps into a wax barrier. The dye moves quickly on silk but sometimes thick fabrics (cotton velvet) require that you work it into the fibers. Mix a variety of colors (all dry lighter), and try these painting techniques: apply one color over another, scrub away portions of a color with paper towels, let one color blend with another, circle a shape with color and let it bleed out until it becomes lighter. Don't be influenced in your color mixings by the light golden color of the waxed lines if you used beeswax. Remember, once the wax is removed, these lines will return to white (or the color of your original fabric).

SETTING THE DYES

The best setting methods for waxed fabric are ironing and steam setting because most of the wax is removed in the process. Batch setting isn't effective because most dye-painted designs are more complex and sections of the fabric dry out before the work is completed so it is impossible to keep the fabric moist for the required 24 hours to properly set the colors.

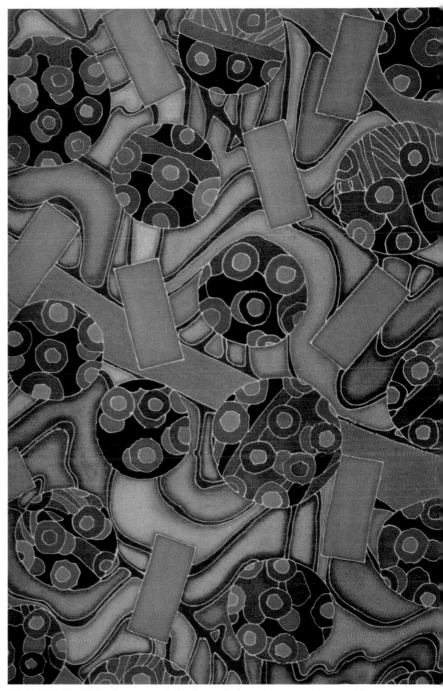

SPACE STREAM #2 by Carolyn A. Dahl. Dye painting with wax resist on silk habotai. Part of the Outer Space silk work series.

REMOVING THE WAX

The amount of wax to remove is less in the dye painting process than in batik as only the design's outlines contain wax. Ironing the fabric will not only heat set it but also remove most of the wax. Protect your work surface with old newspapers (fresh ink transfers when heated). Cover the newspaper with layers of clean newsprint (or packing paper, tissue paper, or all-white paper towels). Lay

Removing the wax by ironing.

the fabric on top of the paper and cover with several layers of clean newsprint. Iron each section slowly at the hottest temperature your fabric can tolerate. Remember you are heat setting the dyes at the same time.

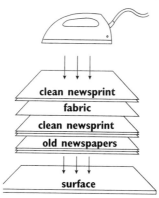

clean newsprint
fabric
clean newsprint
old newspapers

surface

When the papers are saturated with melted wax, change the layers and repeat the process until the paper no longer picks up melted wax. Move to a new area and repeat the process. The melting wax will fume somewhat so have good ventilation in the room and wear a respirator.

Detail of the front of META-MORPHOSIS COAT.

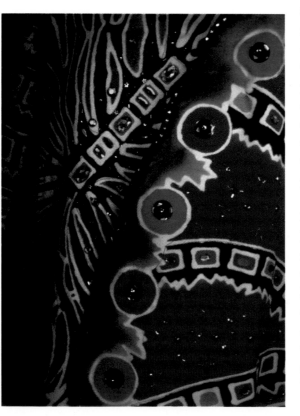

If you steam set your fabric, it's even easier as most of the wax will be absorbed by the paper during steaming. With both setting methods, however, some wax will remain in the fabric (visible as dark rings around the shapes and a slight stiffness to the fibers). However, if I'm making sampler pillow tops, I often leave this wax in the fabric as it gives body to pillows.

However, if you prefer to remove all the wax residue, you will need to have the fabric dry-cleaned. Some dry-cleaners are reluctant to accept hand-painted fabric as they fear the wax and bleeding dye will ruin their solvents, which are reused. If so, you might ask if they would run your fabric through just before they clean their solutions. If you heat set your fabric first, rinse it thoroughly so no dye bleeds out and remove as much of the wax as possible before bringing it in; your fabric shouldn't cause any problems, and the dry-cleaner will soon trust you.

Some will still refuse, however, so if you are the type who likes to have the last word, you might remind them that they owe their business to the very same wax you want removed from your fabric. Back in 1825, Jean Batiste Jolly, a Frenchman, noticed that spilled wax from a paraffin lamp removed some stains on a tablecloth.[6] With that observation, he got the idea to clean clothing using wax as the solvent. Benzene soon replaced paraffin, and later more modern day solvents were developed, but wax started the whole industry. I can't guarantee that this tidbit of cleaning history will change their minds, but it does seem to throw them off balance, giving you time to gather up your precious fabric and make a graceful exit.

If you do not want to use a dry-cleaner, and have a sturdy fabric (not silk), you can try the Indonesian method of wax removal by boiling the fabric and skimming off the melting wax as it rises to the water's surface. I find the process very slow. But if you do use it, do not pour the hot water containing liquid wax down the drain as the wax could collect in your pipes. Instead, allow the water to cool and the wax will solidify into an easily removed sheet. The wax is not reusable as the boiling destroys some of its adhesive properties.

METAMORPHOSIS COAT by Carolyn A. Dahl and Lisa Sharp. Dye painting with wax resist on cotton and rayon velvet, applique, quilting with Sulky® metallic thread, sequins, jewels.

WAX STAMPING

Stamping is the drummer of techniques. Dyes flow quietly and gently into the fabric, but a wooden stamp hits the cloth with a sound. As the stamp repeats across the fabric, the sounds unite into a working rhythm. In the past, rhythm and noise were a normal part of a textile worker's day. Drums and chants often helped to relieve the monotony of the tedious, repetitive work. I can only imagine the cacophony of sounds as workers banged wooden stamps against stones to knock off excess wax, pounded the backside of blocks to transfer paint to the fabric, and smacked the stamps against creaking tables while listening to drumming or chanting. No wonder so many old textiles feel like they are still throbbing with rhythm.

Wax stamps can be made from precut or hand-cut wood shapes covered in felt.

The sound may be quieter now with only one hand stamping per studio. In fact, you may not even be aware of the rhythm when you start the process. At first, the mind slowly directs the hand through each step: dip the stamp in the wax, tap off the excess against the pan, and press the stamp to the cloth. As you continue, however, a faster internal rhythm develops: dip, tap, press, dip, tap, press. You no longer think the process. Your mind falls silent as your body moves to its own trance-like beat.

If you have difficulty feeling the rhythm, you're probably being too timid. Bang the stamp on the table to remind yourself of the technique's noisy tradition. Or, buy the wildest drumming or percussive tape you can find, chase everyone else out of the house, and move to its rhythm until yours awakens.[7]

Detail of wax stamped fabric from TURQUOISE BLOSSOMS by Carolyn A. Dahl (see page 85 for complete work).

MAKING WAX STAMPS

Many found objects can be dipped into hot wax and printed directly. The only consideration is that the object can withstand the heat of the wax. For this reason, wood and metal are traditionally used for wax stamps. Wood will be the material we use, either as a precut or a hand-cut wood shape.

Precut Wood Shapes

Unpainted, precut wood shapes can be found in most hobby or craft stores. Building a collection quickly is easy as they come in numerous shapes (hearts, leaves, snowflakes), numbers, letters, and themes (Christmas, cowboy). To prepare them for use as a wax stamp, you simply trace the shape onto a piece of craft felt, cut out, and glue the felt shape to the wood shape so it will absorb wax; add a handle to the opposite side, and your stamp is ready.

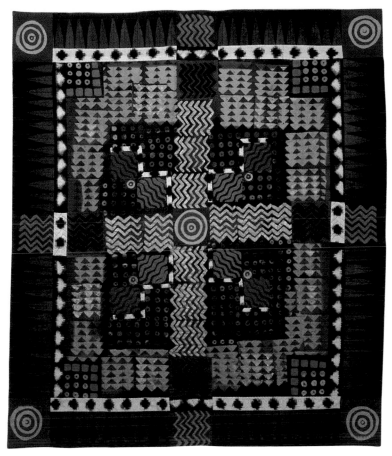

A hand-dyed orange and yellow fabric was wax stamped to preserve areas of the original color and then the open areas were painted a rich brown. Stamp design and fabric by Charlotte Peel.

Hand-cut Wood Shapes

More complex and personal stamps can be made if you design and cut your own wooden shapes. When planning a stamp design, remember that its power often lies in the pattern made when the image is repeated. So test designs you're considering by multiplying the image (trace or photocopy repeatedly and tape together to see the overall effect). If you want a continuous, interlocking stamped pattern like those used on commercial fabrics, refer to the textile design books listed in the chapter notes.[8]

Ann Adams incorporates her wax stamped fabric in her quilt BLOCKED ENERGY. Ann cuts her original stamp designs out of soft balsa wood with a coping or jeweler's saw.

1 Determine the size of your finished stamp. Stamps that are anywhere from a 2" to a 6" square are the easiest to use.

2 Draw your design on tracing paper (design will print in reverse). If your image has multiple parts, number each and allow a little space ($1/8$" to $1/16$") between each section to prevent wax fill in. (a)

a. Draw the design on tracing paper and number the pieces.

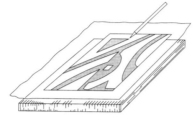

b. Use carbon paper to transfer the stamp design to the wood. Cut out each shape with a saw.

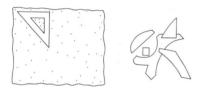

c. Lay the cut out wood pieces on craft felt and trace around each shape. Cut out the shapes drawn on the felt.

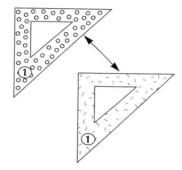

d. Glue each felt shape to the matching wood shape.

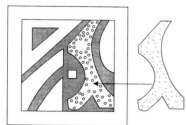

e. Trace the original design onto the support block as a placement guide. Glue the individual felt-covered wood shapes onto the support block matching the shapes to the traced design. Allow to dry.

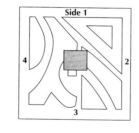

f. Turn the block over. Number all four sides and trace the original design in reverse on the block. Glue on a handle.

3 If you are satisfied with the design, trace it onto the wood from which you intend to cut the individual pieces (thin plywood, Masonite, and balsa wood are good choices). Carbon paper of any type or Sulky® Iron-On Transfer Pens can be used for the transfer. (b)

4 Cut the individual pieces out of the wood with an electric saw (band or scroll saw). If the wood is soft like balsa, a hand saw with a fine blade (coping or jeweler's saw) might be sufficient. Or, if you want to avoid cutting the pieces yourself, you can take them to a woodworker. It helps to design many stamps at once, trace and number all the pieces on the wood yourself, and then request that the lines be followed as precisely as possible. Be sure to have some support blocks cut at the same time so you are ready to mount the pieces immediately.

5 Once all the pieces have been cut out, lay them on white craft felt and trace around the shapes. In order for the wax to stay on the wood for stamping, the surface must be covered with an absorbent material such as felt. (c) Cut out the shapes and glue them onto the matching wood shapes with a heat resistant glue (most wood glues will work). Allow to dry. (d)

6 Now trace the original design again, this time on the support block of wood. Then glue the felt-covered wood shapes onto the support block, matching the numbers of each piece. This will recreate your original design. Allow to dry. (e)

7 Turn the support block over and place a number on each of the four sides. These numbers will serve as guides if you rotate the design as you stamp. It is also helpful to trace the original design on the block. Be sure to reverse the drawing before tracing so it will be in the exact same position as the underside image. Now glue on a handle (small square of wood, thread spool). Your custom-designed stamp is ready to meet the wax. (f)

WAX STAMPING PROCEDURE

Before beginning to stamp with wax, return to page 125 for a review of hot wax safety, temperature control, and set up. The wax mixture (half paraffin and half beeswax), the heat setting methods, and wax removal will also be the same as those described in that section. Whether you use a precut wood stamp or a hand-cut design, the wax stamping procedure will be the same.

Cover the work surface with a thin layer of smooth newspaper. On top of this, place wax paper and then the washed and ironed fabric. Sometimes a short length of fabric needs to be taped at the edges so it won't lift with the stamp.

Submerge the felt portion of the stamp into the hot wax until it absorbs the liquid. Lift the stamp out and tap it against the side of the skillet to remove excess wax, or tilt it and let the overflow run back into the pan. Test the stamp on some scrap fabric. If the waxed image spreads too much, the wax is too hot. If the image appears milky and scratchy, the wax temperature is too low or your stamp is too cold.

When your test images are well defined and the wax is penetrating properly, you are ready to begin. You may choose to stamp in a random pattern or a repeat. If you are doing a repeat pattern, guidelines can be sketched lightly on the fabric. But usually, just starting at a straight line such as the selvage or the top of the fabric will be sufficient for a hand-produced fabric.

Try to develop a rhythm as you work: dip the stamp in the wax, tap off the excess, move quickly to the fabric, and come down straight with the stamp. (If the stamp tilts, wax may run to the edge and drip onto your fabric.) Lift the stamp off and start the procedure again and again.

As with the tjanting tool, avoid crossing over the fabric with a loaded stamp whenever possible. Although a lid or paper towel can be held under the stamp, the stamp's larger size makes the process very awkward and breaks the stamping rhythm. If you're having a problem with drips, you may wish to cover already waxed or unwaxed sections of the fabric with paper as a precaution.

How long to leave the stamp on the fabric and how much pressure to apply must be decided by you. Silk absorbs wax quickly and needs little transfer pressure. A thick cotton may require more pressure as it absorbs wax more slowly. If your stamp design has many large, unbroken surface areas, it will hold a lot of wax. Pressing too hard causes the wax to squish out the sides or fill in smaller design elements. After a few tests, however, you will know what the stamp needs from you by how it is printing.

After the wax is hard, the fabric is ready to paint. Leave the fabric adhered to the wax paper (they will have melted together) and start painting the unwaxed sections of your design.

When the dye is dry, and before heat setting, separate the fabric from the wax paper. This is one of my favorite moments. Not only is the fabric beautiful as it glows with translucent waxed images, but so is the paper that has absorbed the dye.

I never throw beauty away. Instead, I hang the dyed paper in a small round window on my second floor. During the day with the sun outside, it throws color into the room. At night, when it's dark, my lights toss it outside. Neighbors tell me they often walk by at night just to see if a new "stained glass" window has appeared. Knowing they might be out there in the dark, I always leave a light burning. I like the idea of sharing a moment that happened during the process, instead of only the finished product. There may not be a drum sounding in my studio after wax stamping, but I like to think that the color is sending some kind of rhythm into the night.

Precut wood shapes from a craft store were used to stamp designs onto hand-painted or commercially-printed fabric. Then additional colors were added to the background.

When the waxed and painted fabric is separated from the wax paper, both are often colorful and beautiful. The wax paper (on the right) picked up print from the newspaper covering the table, making it the perfect paper to use in Valentine Day collages.

The finished fabric after heat setting, wax removal, and washing.

FRAGMENTS by Carolyn A. Dahl. Sometimes the dye-stained papers that result from the wax and dye process are so beautiful they inspire a new artwork.

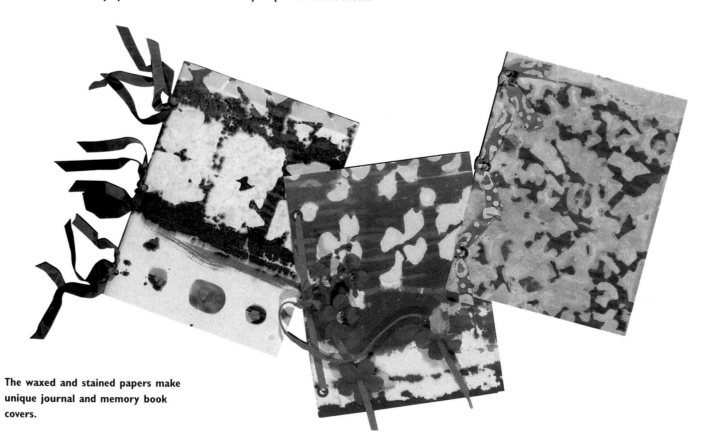

The waxed and stained papers make unique journal and memory book covers.

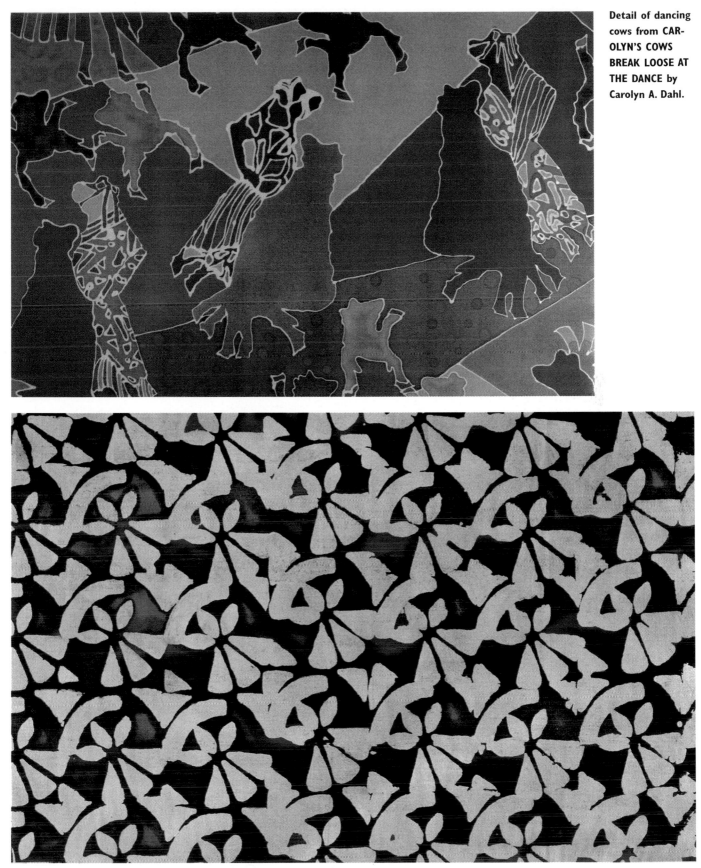

Stamping on white fabric creates a very crisp pattern. The wax may be removed later and additional colors painted into the white areas. Original stamp design and fabric by Mary Ann Willey.

CHAPTER TWELVE

Silk Painting

REMEMBER THE SILKWORM WRAPPED IN HER BED OF SILK dreaming of colors and flowers? In this technique, we answer the dream. We give her old bed, the cocoon now made into silk fabric, the colors of a garden. The painted silk becomes a butterfly.

Silk painting is usually done with French dyes, so called because they originally referred to traditional French colors. Now the term is rather generic indicating dyes that dilute with water and alcohol. Instead of the French dyes, we will substitute fiber-reactive dyes. Some techniques listed in silk painting books will not work as well with fiber-reactive dyes, but the majority can be followed with good results.

The process steps are the same as those given in the Dye Painting with Wax Resist section except that the resist used will not be wax, but a solvent- or water-based resist called gutta. Also, the fabric choice will be limited to silk and the techniques to those that are most effective on silk. As the fabric is a very important component in silk painting, let's cover it first.

TRANSFORMATIONS by Carolyn A. Dahl. Silk painting with fiber-reactive dyes, solvent gutta resist, silk habotai. Photo by Mike McCormick.

SILK FABRIC

The silk most used by fiber artists is habotai (also spelled habotae, habutai). Habotai, which means "soft as down,"[1] is a lightweight, plain-weave fabric with a smooth, lustrous surface that responds well to silk painting techniques. Although it is often called China silk, many sources do not agree that it is exactly the same material.

According to the authors of *Sew Wonderful Silk*, China silk is made from "waste silk,"[2] such as the broken filaments from a pierced cocoon or the end of the cocoon. Because these short fibers have to be spun together to make yarn, the fabric has a different feel from reeled silk. China silk is a very lightweight fabric mainly used for lingerie, scarves, and linings.

Habotai silk, however, is reeled from the cocoon in long unbroken filaments, which are slightly twisted as they are spun into yarn. The result is a heavier, smoother, more opaque silk suitable for clothing and fiber works.

Whether you purchase fabric for silk painting as habotai or China silk, look for yardage with 8, 10, or 12 mommie weight. Mommie (or the Japanese momme, or mm) is an old Chinese term still used today to measure the weight of silk fabric and to remind us of silk's Oriental heritage. *The Art of Painting On Silk* states that "one mommie equals 4.3056 gm (5/32 oz.) in weight to one square metre/yard of fabric … anything under 10 mommie is considered lightweight fabric. …"[3]

Many silks other than habotai may also be used in silk painting as long as the gutta resist can penetrate the fabric. Broadcloth is a good beginner's cloth as it is easy to sew. Crêpe de Chine is a beautiful material, but because it is woven from highly twisted yarns, the dye isn't absorbed as easily and must be worked somewhat into the fabric. Pongee has a slight tooth that holds the dye well, much like good watercolor paper.

Even transparent silks, such as chiffon and organza, take color but require more dye because of their open-weave structure. Painting several layers at once will increase the dye's efficiency. If bold simple shapes are painted, a patterned fabric

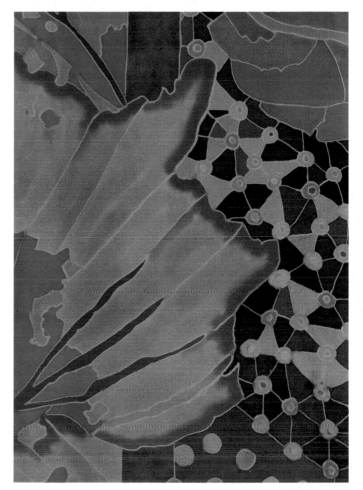

such as a jacquard silk can add an interesting background to the images. And, if you're looking for a rough textured silk that almost resembles cotton, silk noil is a good choice. The little black dots sprinkled across the fabric create a homespun look, but are in reality the remains of the chrysalis caught in the fibers.

One of my favorite fabrics is douppioni silk (or doupion, or the Japanese tamaito). The name is derived from an Italian word for double, because the fabric is made from the silk of two joined cocoons. Maybe it is true that crowding causes the worms to spin together, but I prefer Isabel Wingate's more poetic version: "Two silkworms … have an affinity for each other and want to stay together, so together they spin one cocoon."[4] Although the fabric has a characteristic slub to it, I still think it would be the perfect choice for a Valentine's day dress, or even a wedding dress.

GUTTA RESISTS

COWS by Carolyn A. Dahl. Fiber-reactive dyes on silk.

Gutta means resist in French and comes in two types. The first is solvent soluble and is usually sold as gutta serti (serti means enclosing). The second type is water soluble and called simply gutta, or a water-soluble resist. Both types of gutta are less fluid than wax, seldom drip, and spread very little. Thus your designs can be more detailed and complex than those drawn with hot wax.

Solvent-Soluble Gutta

The solvent-soluble gutta resembles rubber cement and comes from trees of the Sapotacea family found in Borneo, Malaysia, and Sumatra.[5] Occasionally it appears as colle serti, meaning gum or glue resist, but its most common name is gutta serti.

Sometimes the gutta serti you purchase is too thick and will not penetrate your fabric. It must then be thinned with a gutta diluent or thinner sold by the manufacturer, or the recommended solvent (often white spirits). Add the diluent a little at a time, testing the gutta's consistency on scrap fabric until it flows smoothly. If you add too much, leave the cap off the gutta serti until some of the solvent evaporates, which may take a day. Gutta serti does not penetrate heavy silks very well, and you may need to go over the lines on the reverse side of the fabric, apply a wider line, or use a thinner solution.

The gutta serti can be applied with a squeeze bottle fitted with a plastic tip or metal nib (smaller number, smaller hole) or a paper cone (see page 144). Gutta serti colorants may be purchased and added to the clear gutta for colored lines. Some brands can be colored yourself with oil-based paints or printing inks, or you can purchase colored guttas.

The best method to set the dyes after painting is steam setting, as the gutta serti can become sticky when heated with an iron. However, if you do set the dyes with an iron, protect your board and iron as if removing wax. I don't recommend dryer setting, as a solvent would be necessary to remove any gutta should it spot dryer parts, which would be dangerous. Batch setting may be used with solvent-based gutta if the fabric has remained moist.

Solvent-based gutta can only be removed from the fabric by dry-cleaning. Do not, however, dry-clean the colored and metallic guttas as the solvents would dissolve or change the color. As these special guttas are left in the fabric permanently, all lines should be as fine as possible. However, you can avoid the problem by purchasing permanent types of gutta that can be washed or dry-cleaned without damage. (Jacquard has a permanent, water-based metallic resist that comes in eight colors).

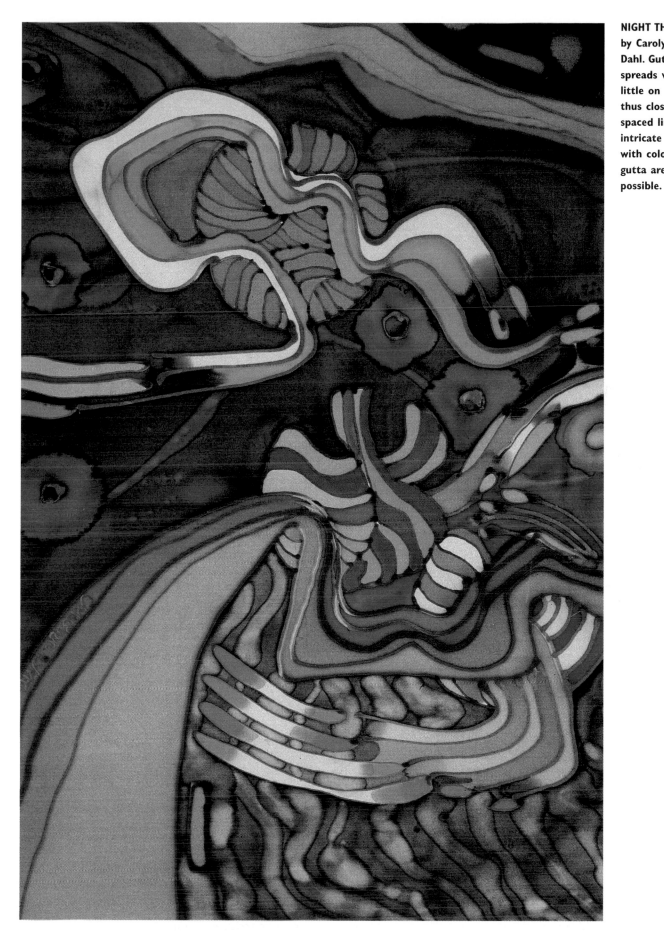

NIGHT THREADS by Carolyn A. Dahl. Gutta serti spreads very little on silk, thus closely spaced lines and intricate designs with colored gutta are possible.

Applying Gutta Serti With a Plastic Bottle

Fill the plastic squeeze bottle with gutta serti completely to the top to eliminate air bubbles. Some bottles come with a plastic tip, others with the metal nib already attached, and some you will need to attach the nib to the plastic cap (wrap a piece of tape around the connection point to prevent separation). Gently squeeze the bottle just enough to bring the gutta up into the spout to eliminate trapped air. Test the consistency on a scrap fabric piece.

If the gutta serti is flowing well, move to your fabric and place the nib where you wish to begin and squeeze gently and steadily. Try for a smooth continuous line with the least amount of stopping and starting. Hold a paper towel in your other hand to wipe the tip which collects excess gutta and sometimes picks up fabric lint. Start at the top of your design and work down, being sure to keep your hands, elbows, and clothing out of the wet resist. If you must stop work for a short period of time, put a thin wire or a straight pin into the hole so the gutta won't clog the opening.

When you finish your work for the day, pour the remaining gutta serti back into the original bottle, clean out the squeeze bottle, and flush the nib with solvent. Allow the gutta serti to dry on the fabric, usually overnight.

Applying Gutta Serti With a Paper Cone

A paper cone, much like a pastry cone for cake decorating, can also be used to apply the gutta serti. A 4" x 6" square of heavy tracing paper, or vellum, is rolled into a cone with the tip in the center of the longest side. Roll the paper tightly, so there's barely a hole in the tip, or none at all. Place a piece of tape over the paper overlaps and around the body of the cone.

Hold the cone upright and fill approximately half full or less with the gutta serti. Carefully fold the top over two or three times to close, and secure with tape so the gutta can't escape when pressure is applied to the cone. If your cone rolling was perfect, you will need to make a tiny hole in the tip with a pin, or snip off a minuscule piece at a slant with a razor blade. Most of the time though, a very small hole will already be present. Don't cut off anything until you've drawn on some test fabric. Usually the existing hole is sufficiently large. Gently squeeze the cone and the gutta will

---

Making a Paper Cone for Gutta Serti.

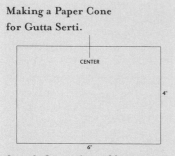

Step 1. Cut a piece of heavy tracing paper 4" x 6". Locate the center of the longest side.

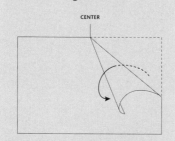

Step 2. Begin rolling the paper, keeping the tip at the center. Roll tightly to make a very fine tip.

Step 3. Wrap a piece of tape around the cone to secure the paper overlap. Fill the cone ½ full with gutta serti.

Step 4. Roll down the top of the cone and close securely with tape to prevent gutta leakage. Cut a tiny amount off the tip if necessary.

JUNGLE FLOWER (detail) by Carolyn A. Dahl. Very fine gutta lines are possible when a paper cone is used to apply the resist. One of the floral silk paintings commissioned by Tiffany and Co.

start to flow. Hold the cone in a fairly vertical position and draw it gently across the fabric, moving slowly.

Although using a cone may sound more difficult than using a plastic squeeze bottle, the cone has several advantages: a much finer line can be drawn, unused gutta can be left in the cone in a plastic bag as there are no nibs to clog, and fewer bubbles occur because the cone doesn't suck in air like a plastic bottle when you release the pressure. Best of all, no clean up is required as the used cones can be discarded. I also find that if I am drawing a very complex pattern that may take most of the day to complete, the cone doesn't tire my hand muscles as much as a squeeze bottle.

Water-Soluble Gutta

If you do not choose to use the traditional gutta serti, many water-soluble guttas, or resists, are available in ready-to-use plastic bottles. Unlike gutta serti, water-soluble resists can be removed with water after the fabric has been heat set, but that also means they can be washed off the fabric with any water, including dyes. Thus some precautions must be followed to prevent the dyes from dissolving the resist lines.

Before beginning your design transfer, test your brand of resist and line width on the fabric you intend to use. Most water-soluble resists were developed to be used with particular dyes or fabric paints (you can color some by adding dye or paint). As we are substituting fiber-reactive dye

solutions that contain auxiliary chemicals, always do a test strip to be sure that the resist you've chosen will create a strong barrier.

Use only lightweight silks and allow the resist to dry completely before painting. Many instructions say that the silk may be painted while the resist is still wet, but it doesn't work well for me. Either the dye breaks through the moist line, or I smear it with my brush.

When painting, do not overload the brush and flood the fabric with liquid. Paint in a rather dry style, applying the color to the center of the shape and allowing it to bleed to the resist line. Avoid painting over the lines, or layering many colors, as the liquid may weaken the resist and cause feathering.

As water-soluble resists do not become tacky like gutta serti, the fabrics may be heat set by ironing. Avoid batch setting, and if you steam set, increase your line width and shorten the steaming time (check with the manufacturer if their brand can be steamed at all). The lengthened exposure to moisture could cause some line edges to erode and allow the dye to seep into reserved areas. After heat setting, some brands harden in the fabric slightly making removal difficult. Try soaking the fabric in white vinegar which should soften the resist and make it easier to wash off.

The lines of a drawing under the silk can be easily traced with the metal tip of a plastic squeeze bottle filled with resist.

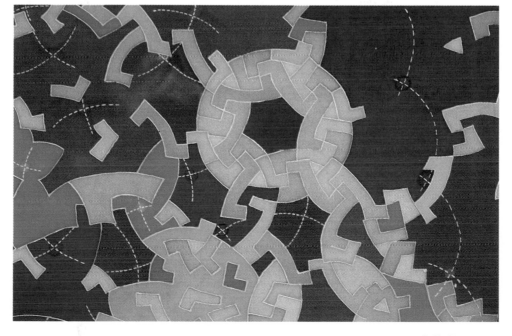

SPINNING by Carolyn A. Dahl. Gutta resists are the best choice for geometric designs as they spread less than wax.

PAINTING TECHNIQUES

One of the challenges in silk painting is achieving a smooth background, free of stop and start lines. As most silk designs are more complex, going around the many shapes requires a quick pace. Start by mixing a sufficient quantity of dye so you don't run out. Select the largest brush possible. Work in one direction trying to end each pass at the selvage and not in the center of the fabric. Keep the edges wet and work quickly. If you do get a hard edge, rub it immediately, which will often blend it or at least make it less conspicuous.

IRIS GARDEN by Carolyn A. Dahl. One of the floral silk paintings commissioned by Tiffany and Co.

As liquid dye is similar to other water media, many of the silk painting techniques are derived from watercolor methods. As you apply the liquid color to the silk, you will begin to understand why the following are silk painters' favorite techniques.

- Touch a dye-loaded brush to the center of a shape or an edge of a shape and allow the dye to spread and lighten.
- Paint a second color (or pure chemical water) over an almost dry color to create patterns inside a shape.
- Blot or rub out the center of a newly painted color to create a lighter area. (See pages 127 and 131.)
- Layer one color over another for a softly blended effect.

THE ROSE by Carolyn A. Dahl. One of the floral silk paintings commissioned by Tiffany and Co

NASTURTIUMS by Carolyn A. Dahl. One of the floral silk paintings commissioned by Tiffany and Co.

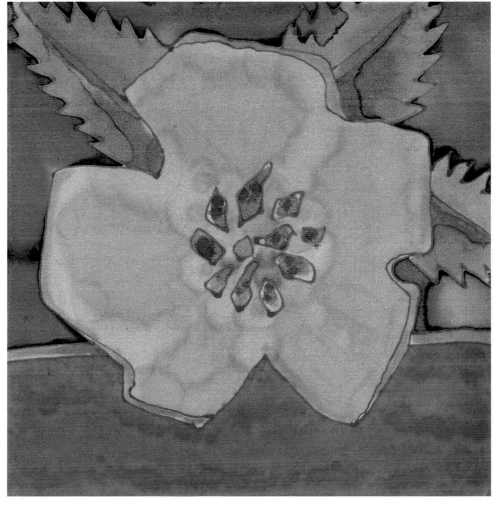

Overlaying one color with another on a simple flower shape gives a softly blended effect.

SALT EFFECTS

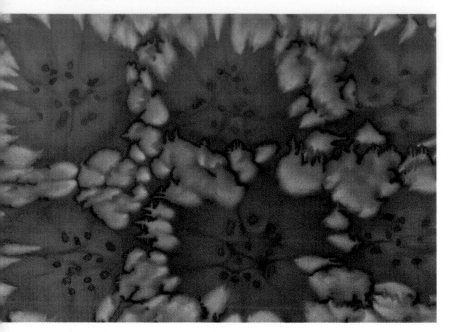

Rock salt placed in the wet dye and allowed to dry results in wonderful dark crystal shapes.

Salt patterns on silk have almost become the silk painters' trademark. Although the patterns look complex and time consuming, the process is simple. The salt is placed on the fabric while the dye is wet. As the salt absorbs liquid from the surrounding area, the color is pulled into distinctive patterns. Even though the actual process may be easy, some factors influence the salt's effectiveness and the final results.

Fabric and Color

One of the reasons habotai silk is so often used in silk painting is that it yields beautiful salt patterns. Heavier silks and cotton can also be used, but the results are not as dramatic. The fabric should be stretched tightly over a frame while painting and salting, so the dye doesn't pool in low spots and dissolve the salt.

Select white or pastel-colored fabric and dark-to-medium dye colors (forest green, purple, teal blue, raspberry or magenta, navy blue, and some browns) to create strong contrasts.

Salt Type and Placement

Salt comes in various crystal sizes. Each will give a slightly different effect depending on its size, additives, and impurities. Experiment with whatever type you find: uniodized table salt, coarse Kosher salt, rock salt (used for making ice cream), canning and pickling salt, and water softener salts. The most frequently used salt is regular table salt which has a smaller crystal. Avoid iodized salt as iodine is a metal that can dull the dye's color. Although rock salt has impurities that can also affect the color, I still use it because its large crystal size is perfect for some patterns.

To understand how each crystal reacts with your fabric, make a salt sampler. Stretch the fabric on a frame and draw large squares with the gutta. Try a different color and salt in each square. Use only a few grains for a widely-spaced pattern and then try densely-packed crystals for a spotted mass. Once you know what each crystal type does on your fabric, you can decide if you want an all over sprinkling of one salt, hand placing of individual chunks, or a mixture of salts for an interactive pattern.

Moisture in the Fabric and the Salt

Only experience and observation will tell you exactly when to drop the salt onto the wet fabric. If you add the salt too soon after painting, it will dissolve in the excess moisture. If you wait too long, the dye locks into the fibers and the salt will be unable to move it.

Watch for the moment that the fabric's sheen changes from the look of water to simply being wet, then act quickly. If in doubt, salt sooner rather than later. When I'm doing large areas of color, such as backgrounds, I paint with my right hand and immediately salt with my left.

While the fabric must be wet, the salt must be completely dry if it is to move the color by absorption. Salt is hygroscopic and will collect moisture from the environment, so always store the salt you intend to use for dyeing in a dry place. Before beginning to work, hold it in your hand to determine if it is moist. If so, put it in a shallow pan in a warm oven until dry.

Removing Salt

Allow the salt to dry on the fabric undisturbed. Be sure that it is completely dry before attempting to remove the remaining salt crystals, but don't wait too long or they will become crusty and difficult to remove.

Invert the frame over a large garbage can or a layer of newspapers to collect the dye-stained salt. Shake or lightly tap the backside of the stretched fabric, which will cause most of the crystals to pop off. Avoid brushing the salt crystals across the fabric with your hands. If one crystal still retains moisture, you could streak your fabric with unwanted color.

Hold your frame at an angle. Any glint of light could indicate crystals still stuck to the fabric. Remove remaining salt with your fingernails, or by a gentle rubbing with a scrap piece of clean silk fabric which won't abrade the surface. Try to remove as much salt as possible before the fabric is heat set. The fabric will feel very stiff where the salt has been, but the softness will return after washing.

Setting Salt-Patterned Fabric

Because the pattern is achieved by allowing the salt to dry at its own pace, setting by batching should be avoided as it would interfere with the salt's natural timing. So salt-patterned fabrics should be heat set by ironing or steaming.

If steaming, some precautions should be taken to avoid the problems salt can create in the moisture-filled environment of a steamer. Even though your fabric will be completely dry and all visible traces of salt removed, the areas where the salt was will still contain some residue.

As the steam surrounds the fabric, the remaining salt will attract moisture. Your colors could run or bleed through the protective paper wrap and onto other areas of the fabric. To prevent this, always put an additional layer or two of paper over the salted areas before rolling up the bundle for steaming.

LENA'S IRIS by Carolyn A. Dahl. The salt-patterned background adds interest and depth to a single flower composition.

SILK PAINTING WITH PIGMENTS

Detail of COWS by Carolyn A. Dahl.

If you would like to try the resist and silk painting method, but prefer to substitute pigments for the fiber-reactive dyes, I'd recommend Dyena-Flow by Jacquard. The product leaves the silk soft to the touch, works well with salt techniques, is fixed by ironing or clothes dryer or an air fixer that is added to the color, works on any fiber content, and is easy for beginners as the paint can be used right from the jar.

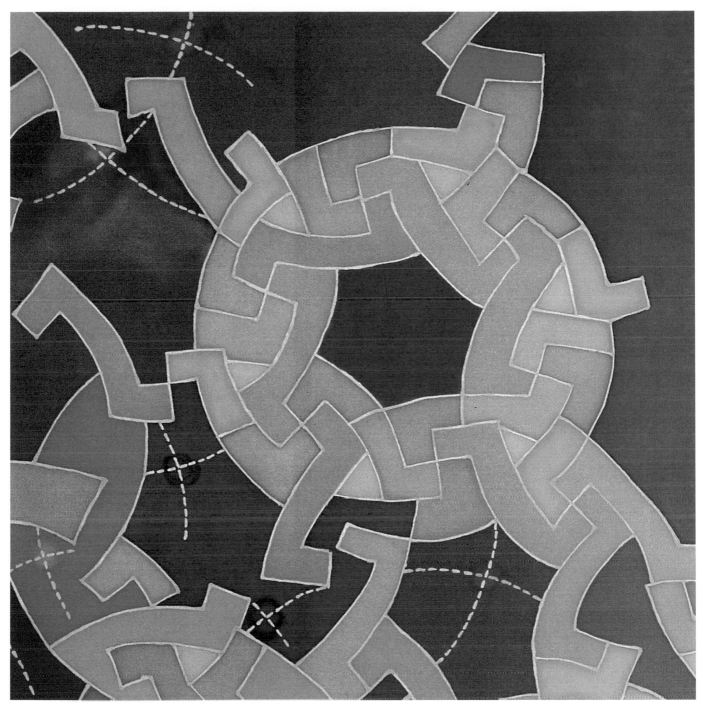

Detail of **SPINNING** by Carolyn A. Dahl. Gutta resist and fiber-reative dyes on silk.

Closing

IN OUR TECHNOLOGICAL SOCIETY, much of our cloth is designed by computers and colored by fast-paced machines. We have fabric that is called "active" as it adjusts to our body temperature or changes color. We are already wearing materials that were once industrial interfacings or space flight protection gear. Perhaps, when we want a new wardrobe in the future, a heat gun will fuse the fabrics together instead of a sewing machine, and we'll dissolve our outdated clothes in water.

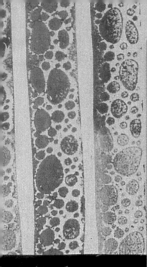

Yet for all the wonders of technology, I believe there will always be a place for hand-designed fabric and those who produce it. Perhaps even a need for it. If you hold commercial fabric in one hand and your hand-dyed fabric in the other, only one will have a heartbeat. Somehow for all their efficiency and innovation, machines still can't speak to whatever it is in us that makes us human. Fabric filled with the mark of a soul and the mark of a hand will always be important, no matter how far the definition of fabric stretches.

ABOUT THE AUTHOR

Carolyn A. Dahl has appeared on the Carol Duvall show, Simply Quilts (Home and Garden Television), and Sew Creative (PBS). Her dyed and painted textiles and paper vessels have been shown in many museums and art centers, in galleries throughout the country, and in Holland and Italy. Many magazines and 10 books have featured her work. She lives in Houston, Texas.

BLIND DRAWING #2 by Carolyn A. Dahl. Painted cotton, free-style machine stitching, Egyptian Temple painting stamp © Uptown Design Co.

FOOTNOTES

CHAPTER ONE
The Cloth: Bowing to the White
1 Gaffey, Theresa. "Cotton," Flying Needle, February 1993.
2 Ibid
3 Ibid.
4 Feltwell, Dr. John. *The Story of Silk*. New York: St. Martin's Press Inc. 1990.
5 Ibid.
6 Ibid.
7 Ibid.
8 Nuttall, Carol Anne. "Beginning With Raw Silk," *Shuttle, Spindle and Dyepot*. Vol. XXVI, No. 1, Issue 101, Winter 94-95.
9 Wingate, Isabel B. *Textile Fabrics and Their Selection*. New Jersey: Prentice-Hall Inc. 1964.
10 Ibid.

CHAPTER TWO
The Colorants
1 Robinson, Stuart. *A History of Dyed Textiles*. Great Britain: Studio Vista Limited, 1969.
2 Sandburg, Gosta. *Indigo Textiles, Technique and History*. North Carolina: Lark Books, 1989.
3 Tompson, Frances and Tony. *Synthetic Dyeing*. Newton Abbot Devon: David and Charles Craft Book, 1987.
4 Ibid.
5 Brusatin, Manlio. *A History of Colors*. Massachusetts: Shambhala Inc., 1991.
6 Books on color: *The Art of Color* by Johannes Itten; *Blue and Yellow Don't Make Green* by Michael Wilcox; *A Color Notation* by A.H. Munsell; and *Interaction of Color* by Josef Albers. Many watercolor books are also excellent for color mixing ideas as watercolor and dyes are both transparent mediums.

CHAPTER FOUR
Water Drop Patterns
1 Ferron, Miquel. *Airbrush Painting*. New York: Watson-Guptill, 1988.
2 If you are unable to find Preval® sprayers in paint or auto supply stores, contact: Precision Valve Corporation, Preval Sprayer Division, P.O. Box 309, Yonkers, NY 10702.

CHAPTER FIVE
Nature's Patterns
1 Little, Robert W. *Nature Printing*. Pennsylvania: Pickwick-Morecraft, Inc., 1984.
2 Hochberg, F.G., "Gyotax," Nature Printing Society Newsletter, Vol. XIII, #1, March 1990.
3 For information on membership: The Nature Printing Society, 8821 Interlachen Rd., Lake Shore, MN 56468. E-mail: sonjanps@uslink.net

4 Information taken from the brochure of Screen Process Mfg. Co. (supplier of Inkodyes).

CHAPTER SEVEN
Compression Dyeing
1 Wada, Yoshiko; Mary Kellogg Rice; and Jane Barton. Shibori, *The Inventive Art of Japanese Shaped Resist Dyeing*. NY: Kodansha, 1983.

CHAPTER EIGHT
Heat-Transfer Dyes
1 Scott, Guy. *Transfer Printing onto Man-Made Fibers*. MA: Charles T. Branford. Co. 1977.

CHAPTER TEN
Destructive Patterns
1 Robinson, Stuart. *A History of Dyed Textiles*. London: Studio Vista Limited, 1969.

CHAPTER ELEVEN
Wax Patterns
1 Anderson, F. *Tie-dyeing and Batik*. London: Octopus Books, 1974.
2 Kretvitsky, Nik. *Batik Art and Craft*. New York: Van Nostrand and Reinhold Co. No date given.
3 Singer, Margo and Mary Spyrou. *Textile Arts Multicultural Traditions*. Pennsylvania: Chilton Book Co., 1989.
4 Belfer, Nancy. *Designing In Batik and Tie Dye*. Massachusetts: Davis Publications, Inc., 1972.
5 Anderson, F. Ibid.
6 Tortora, Phyllis G. *Understanding Textiles*. New York: Macmillan Publishing Co., 1987.
7 I have enjoyed these drumming and percussion tapes. "Bones" by Gabrielle Roth and the Mirrors; "Thunderdrums" by Scott Fitzgerald; and any Mickey Hart tape.
8 For information on how to turn any image into a repeat pattern, refer to these textile design books: *Design Your Own Repeat Patterns*, V. Ann Waterman, Dover Publications; and *Textile Print Design*, Richard Fisher and Dorothy Wolfthal, Fairchild Publications.

CHAPTER TWELVE
Silk Painting
1 Brown, Gail, *Sensational Silk*. Portland Oregon: Palmer/Pletsch Associates, 1982.
2 Arrants, Cheryl with Jan Asbjornsen *Sew Wonderful Silk*. Seattle: Sew Wonderful, 1980.
3 *The Art of Painting on Silk* Vol. 3 Fashions. Kent: Search Press Ltd. 1990 (no author listed).
4 Wingate, Isabel B., *Textile Fabrics and Their Selection*. New Jersey: Prentice-Hall, Inc. 1964.
5 Kennedy, Jill and Jane Varall, *Painting On Silk*. London: Drayad Press Ltd., 1988.

SUPPLY SOURCES

Most dyeing and painting supplies can be purchased or ordered from your local art supply, fabric store, or craft retailer. If you are unable to locate a hard-to-find product in your area, or need a specialized material, contact the manufacturers and mail order companies listed below. For a full range of their products, consult their catalogs or Web sites.

All Night Media, Inc.
Box 2835, Norcross, GA 30091
(800) 842-4197 www.plaidonline.com
Rubber Stamps

Binney and Smith
1100 Church Ln., P.O. Box 431
Easton, PA 18044-0431 (800) CRAYOLA
www.crayola.com
Crayola Fabric Crayons

CARL Manufacturing
1862 South Elmhurst Rd.
Mount Prospect, IL 60056
(847) 956-0730 www.carl-products.com
Iron-Transfer Dyeing Paper

Center Enterprises, Inc.
P.O. Box 331361, West Hartford, CT 06133
(800) 542-2214 www.centerenterprises.com
Stamp and Press Fabric-Transfer Ink Pads

Clearsnap Inc.
P.O. Box 98, Anacortes, WA 98221
(800) 448-4862 www.clearsnap.com
MagicStamp®, Rollagraphs

Createx/Color Craft, Ltd.
14 Airport Park Rd., East Granby, CT 06026
(800) 243-2712 www.createxcolors.com
Liquid Pure Pigments, dyes, paints

Dharma Trading Co.
P.O. Box 150916, San Rafael, CA 94915
(800) 542-5227 www.dharmatrading.com
Fiber-reactive dyes (MX, H, H Liquid), Compressed Sponges, Bleach Stop, Synthetic Bleach Thickener, Versatex Air Brush Ink, Flexible Printing Plate, all brands of fabric paint and dyes.

E.K. Success Ltd.
P.O. Box 1141, Clifton, NJ 07014
(800) 524-1349 www.eksuccess.com
ZIG Textile Markers

Fred B. Mullett Co.
P.O. Box 94502, Seattle, WA 98124
(206) 624-5723 www.fredbmullett.com
Fish Print Rubber Stamps

Gumbo Graphics
c/o Stamp Francisco
308 SE 271st Ct., Camas, WA 98607
(360) 210-4031 www.stampfrancisco.com
Rubber Stamps

Hampton Art Stamps
19 Industrial Blvd., Medford, NY 11763
(800) 229-1019 www.hamptonart.com
Rubber Stamps

Hot Potatoes
2805 Columbine Pl., Nashville, TN 37204
(615) 269-8002 www.hotpotatoes.com
Rubber Stamps

Inkadinkado
61 Holton St., Woburn, MA 01801
(800) 888-4652 www.inkadinkado.com
Rubber Stamps

John Marshall: Works in Fabric
The Old Flour Mill
P.O. Box 115, Covelo, CA 95428
(707) 983-6636 www.johnmarshall.to
Shinshi, Harite, Oriental Supplies

Ken Brown Stamps
P.O. 567, Saxtons River, VT 05154
(800) 553-5031
www.stampusa.com/artists/ken.htm
Rubber Stamps

Krause Publications
700 East State St., Iola, WI 54990-0001
(800) 258-0929 www.krause.com
Books

NASCO
901 Janesville Ave., P.O. Box 901
Fort Atkinson, WI 53538
(800) 558-9595 www.eNASCO.com
Rubber Blocks, Flexible Printing Plates, Carving Tools

Pelle's See Thru Stamps
From Purrfection, 12323 99th Ave. NE
Arlington, WA 98223 (800) 691-4293
www.purrfection.com
Rubber Stamps

Posh Impressions
22600-A Lambert St., Suite 706
Lake Forest, CA 92630   (800) 421-7674
www.poshimpressions.com
Rubber Stamps

PRO Chemical and Dye Inc.
P.O. Box 14, Somerset, MA 02726
(800) 228-9393   www.prochemical.com
Fiber-Reactive Powdered Dyes, PROPaste Mix, PROsperse Dyes, Anti-Chlor, Tjantings, Wax, Guttas, Synthrapol

Ranger Industries
15 Park Rd., Tinton Falls, N.J. 07724
(800) 244-2211   www.rangerink.com
Alphabet stamps

Red Pearl Stamps
P.O. Box 94502, Seattle, WA 98124
Rubber Stamp Seal Designs

Rubber Stampede
2550 Pellissier Pl., Whittier, CA 90601
(800) 632-8386
www.rubberstampede.com *(Rubber Stamps)*
www.deltacraft.com *(Delta Stencils)*

Rupert, Gibbon and Spider, Inc.
P.O. Box 425, Healdsburg, CA 95448
(800) 442-0455
www.jacquardproducts.com
Lumiere Metallic Fabric Paint, Permanent Metallic Gutta, Jacquard Discharge Paste, Dyes, Chemicals, Tools, Dye-Na-Flow

Screen Process Supplies Mfg. Co.
530 MacDonald Ave, Richmond, CA 94801
(510) 235-8330
Inkodyes

Silkpaint Corporation
P.O. Box 18, 18220 Waldron Dr.
Waldron, MO 64092   (800) 563-0074
www.silkpaint.com
Fiber-Etch® and Devoré fabrics

Speed Stitch, Inc. (Sulky of America)
3113 Broadpoint Dr., Punta Gorda, FL 33983
(800) 874-4115   www.speedstitch.com
Sulky® Iron-On Transfer Pens

Stamp Oasis
4750 W. Sahara Ave., Las Vegas, NV 89102
(702) 878-6474   www.stampoasis.com
Rubber Stamps

Stampendous, Inc.
1240 N. Red Gum, Anaheim, CA 92806-1820
(800) 869-0474   www.stampendous.com
Rubber Stamps

Testfabrics
P. O. Box 26, West Pittston, PA 18643
(570) 603-0432   www.testfabrics.com
Prepared-for-Dyeing Fabrics

Thai Silks
252 State St., Los Altos, CA 94022
(800) 722-SILK (outside CA)
(800) 221-SILK (CA)
www.thaisilks.com
Habotai scarves, silk yardage

The Stamp Pad Co. Inc.
P.O. Box 43, Big Lake, MN 55309
(800) 634-3717   www.stampin.com
Rubber Stamps

The Stencil Company
28 Castlewood Dr., Cheektowaga, NY 14227
(716) 656-9430   www.quiltingstencils.com
Quilting Stencils

Uptown Design Co.
1000 Town Center Suite 1
Browns Point, WA 98422   (800) 888-3212
www.UptownDesign.com
Rubber Stamps

WTP Inc.
P.O. Box 937, Coloma, MI 49038
(800) 521-0731   www.wtp-inc.com
Holographic Disks, Molded Plastic Fish Eyes

INDEX

A

Acetate rayon, 16, 88
Acid dyes, 21
Activator mixture, 25, 27
Adams, Ann, 135
Air brush ink, 34, 44, 46
Air Pen™, 120
Alginate, 27
Alkali activators
    activator mixture, 23
    baking soda, 23
    recipes, 25, 27
    soda ash, 23
Anderson, F., 128
Animal sea sponges, 67, 68
Auchard, Betty, 51
Azeta cloth, for devoré, 118, 120
Azoic dyes, 21

B

Background, painting, 23, 54, 103
Baking soda (bicarbonate of soda), 23, 25, 27
Batch setting/batching
    compression dyeing, 76
    fiber-reactive dyes, 25, 28
    water drop patterns, 48
Batik
    Indonesian, 122, 127
    wax resist, 123, 125
Beeswax, 125, 131
Beginner's techniques, black and-white, 37
Binders, in fabric paint, 33
Binding and dyeing, 74, 79
Birthday cloth, 96
Black-and-white transformations, 36
    beginner's techniques, 37
    color bands and blotches, 41
    coloring book, 38
    linear bleed, 40
    selective focus, 39
    sprayed patterns, 40
    zebra jacket, 37
Bleach patterns, 110
    chili cloth, 116–117
    discharge, 111
    fabrics, 113
    neutralize, 114
    Nuclear Forest #3, 112
    procedures, 115
    test samples, 114
Blind drawing portrait, 94, 95
Bombyx Mori, 13
Bone print, 58
Boser, Brett, 95
Braiding and dyeing, 74, 77
Burn-out/devoré, 118–121

C

Canning pot steamer, 28–29
Caustic soda (sodium hydroxide), 11
Cellulose sponges, 67–68

Chemical water
    adding dye, 25
    preparation, 25
    Procion® H series, 24
    Procion® MX series, 23
    purpose, 26
Chiffon silk, 79, 141
Child collaboration portrait, 94, 95
Chili cloth, discharge, 116–117
China silk, 13, 58, 141
Chlorine bleach, 113–115
Clothes dryer setting
    heliotropic, 65
    Procion® H series, 24
    rain cloth, 44
    recipes, 25, 28
    solvent-soluble gutta, 142
Color bands and blotches, 41
Color, mixing dyes, 25, 26–27, 62–63
Colorants
    dyes. See Dyes
    dyes vs. paints, 22, 30
    fabric paints. See Fabric paints
    history, 20–21
    silk painting with pigments, 150–151
    Underwater, 20
Coloring book technique, 38
Compression dyeing, 74–75
    binding, 74, 79
    braiding, 74, 77
    Earth Strata #1 and #2, 81
    folding and pleating, 46, 74, 81
    gathering, 74
    Inkodyes, 63
    knotting, 74, 78
    procedure, 75–76
    scrunching. See Scrunching and dyeing
    Shibori Storm, 74
    Silk Ensemble, 80
    stitching. See Stitching and dyeing
    twisting, 74, 78
Cotton, 9
    activating dye solution, 25
    cellulose sponges, 67–68
    corduroy, 11
    for dispersed dyeing, 88
    fish bone print, 58
    history, 10
    overview, 9
    purchasing, 11
    washing and storing, 17
Crayon cloth, 93
Crazy quilts, 12
Crêpe de Chine, 141

D

Dahl, Carolyn A.
    background, 153
    introduction, 6–7
Dauber (tampo), 58

de Chardonnet, Count Hilaire, 16
De Plasse, Noel, 87
Destructive patterns, 110
    chili cloth, 116–117
    devoré/burn-out, 118–121
    discharge patterns, 111–112
    discharge procedure, 113–115
    Nuclear Forest #3, 110, 111, 112
Devoré/burn-out, 118–121
Direct application techniques
    chemical water, 26
    compression dyeing, 75
    defined, 7, 22
    heliotropic, 63
    Procion® H series, 24
    Procion® MX series, 23
Direct printing method, 56–57
Discharge
    agent, bleach, 113–115
    bleach patterns, 111–112
    paste, 115
    procedure, 113–115
Disperse dyes, 21. See also Heat-transfer dyes (dispersed)
Douppioni silk, 141
Dry-cleaning, 132, 142
Dye painting with wax resist, 123–125
Dye-saturated paper sheets, 88, 96–98
Dyeing
    compression. See Compression dyeing
    immersion, 23, 24, 26
    sponging, 68
Dyes. See also Heat-transfer dyes (dispersed)
    acid, 21
    azoic, 21
    disperse, 21. See also Heat-transfer dyes (dispersed)
    disposal, 29
    fiber-reactive. See Fiber-reactive dyes
    French, 140
    heat-transfer. See Heat-transfer dyes (dispersed)
    heliotropic, 62
    history, 21
    Inkodyes, 51, 62, 63
    metal-complex, 21
    natural, 21
    paints vs., 22, 30
    paste, 25, 115
    PROsperse, 97–99
    reactive, 21
    sun-reactive, 62
    synthetic, 21
    vat, 21, 62
Dynamiting silk, 12

E

Edison, Thomas, light bulb, 10
Elliott, Connie, 79
Erasers, carving, 101, 104

de Chardonnet... (cont.)

Extender
    fabric paint, 33
    heliotropic dyes, 63

F

Fabric paints
    Birthday Breakdown, 33
    devoré/burn-out technique, 119
    dyes vs., 22, 30
    fish print stamps, 59
    leaf printing, 52
    Nature Spirit, 35
    overview, 30–35
    Shaman's Coat, 32
    Space Age Ethnic, 30, 31
    sponging, 68
    wax patterns, 131
Fabric-transfer crayons, 93
Fabric-transfer ink pads, 88–91
Fabrics
    blends, 88
    cotton. See Cotton
    devoré/burn-out technique, 120
    hand-designed, 152
    rain cloth, 43–44
    rayon. See Rayon
    ready-to dye, 19
    silk. See Silk
    spray cloth, 45–48
    synthetics for dispersed dyeing, 87, 88
    water drop yardage, 49
Farm-Heumann, Susan, 108–109
Fiber-Etch®, 118, 119
Fiber-reactive dyes, 7
    compression dyeing, 75
    Procion® H. See Procion® H series
    Procion® MX. See Procion® MX series
    recipes. See Recipes for fiber-reactive dyes
    safety precautions, 24, 29
Fish printing
    direct printing method, 56–57
    eyes, painting & holographic, 57
    Gyotaku, 58
    indirect printing method, 56, 58
    stamps, 59–60
Fixer, 23, 27
Flexible printing plate, 100, 101, 103
Folding and dyeing, 46, 74, 81
Franklin, Benjamin
    kite, 12
    leaf printing, 51
Free motion stitching, 63
French dyes, 140

G

Gutta resists
    clothes dryer setting, 28
    colored, 142
    Cows, 142

Jungle Flower, 144
metallic, 142
Night Threads, 143
solvent-soluble (gutta serti, colle serti), 142–145
Spinning, 145
water-soluble, 142, 145
Gyotaku, 58

H

Habotai silk, 58, 141, 148
Hand-cut stamps, 100
    Artful Cloth, 100, 101
    Chinese seals, 60
    designing, 102
    erasers, 101, 104
    flexible printing plate, 100, 101, 103
    MagicStamp® (PenScore ™), 69, 71–72, 108–109
    materials, 101
    polystyrene plates, 100
    rubber blocks, 101, 105–107.
        See also Rubber stamps
    sheet foam, 69, 100, 101, 103
    wood, 134, 135
Harite, 124, 130
Heat setting
    batching. *See* Batch setting/batching
    clothes dryer. *See* Clothes dryer setting
    fish print stamps, 60
    iron. *See* Ironing, heat setting
    steaming. *See* Steam setting
    sun printing, 65
Heat-transfer dyes (dispersed), 86
    Bananas And Butterflies, Pens and Pears, 91
    Birthday Card for Candace, 96
    Birthday Party for Aaron, 96
    Blind Drawing #3, 95
    And The Cats Jumped Over The Moon, 89
    dye-saturated paper sheets, 88, 96–97
    Eye In Eye #3, 97
    fabric, 88
    fabric-transfer crayons, 93
    fabric-transfer ink pads, 88–91
    Fall Monarchs, 86
    forms of dye, 88
    Growing Into My Grandmother's Eyes, 99
    heat source, 88
    history, 87
    Iron-On Transfer Pens, 94–95, 98
    mini-yardage, 89–90, 92
    paper, 87
    portrait of uncle in uniform, 98
    powdered dispersed dyes, 97–99
Heat-transfer inks, 59
Heliotropic (sun-reactive, Inkodyes), 61
    Butterfly Dancers, 63
    color mixing, 62–63
    dyes, 62
    Inkodyes, 51, 62, 63

needlepoint canvas, 104
photogram process, 63–64
washing, 65

I

Immersion dyeing, 23, 24, 26
Indirect printing method, 56, 58
Indonesia
    batik, 122, 127
    Tritik, 82
    wax lines and mood, 128
    wax removal method, 132
    wax resist recipes, 124
Ink
    airbrush, 34, 44, 46
    heat-transfer, 59
    Inkodyes, 51, 62, 63
Iron-On Transfer Pens
    portraits, 94–95, 98
    rubber blocks, 105
    wax patterns, 126
    wax stamping, 136
Ironing, heat setting
    gutta resists, 145
    heat-transfer dyeing, 88, 92
    Procion® H series, 24
    rain cloth, 44
    recipes, 25, 28
    rubber blocks, 105
    salt-patterned fabrics, 149
    solvent-soluble gutta, 142
    wax patterns, 131, 132

J

Jacquard silk fabric, 141, 142
Japan
    gyotaku, 58
    history of due pot, 21
    Naikan philosophy, 8–9
    Shibori, 74–75
    silk, 13
Jetton, Mark, 88
Johnson, Melody, 45
Jolly, Jean Batiste, 132

K

Knotting and dyeing, 74, 78

L

Leaf printing, 51–55
Lee, Iris, 118, 119
Lindveit, Winnie, 56–57, 58
Linear bleed technique, 40
Liquid H dyes, 26
Loading silk, 12
Lumieré metallic paint, 22, 52

M

Machado, Ann Bae, 57, 58
Machine washing silk, 18
MagicStamp® (PenScore ™), 69, 71–72, 108–109
Mandeville, Sir John, 10
Markers, textile, 55, 88, 126
Memory cloth, 70–73
Mercerization, 11
Metal-complex dyes, 21

Metallic
    gutta resists, 142
    salts, 12
Microcrystalline wax (sticky wax), 125
Mildew, prevention, 17
Mini-yardage, heat transfer, 89–90, 92
Mirror image, stitched, 83
Mixing colors, 131
Moldable-foam printing, 66
    Don't Throw Away My Dolls, 71, 73
    For Hunter Rose And All The Children, 70
    memory cloth, 70–73
    overview, 69
Mommie, silk weight, 141
Monagum (starch), 115
Mullett, Fred, 59–60

N

Naikan philosophy, 8–9
Natural dyes, 21
Nature's patterns, 50
    fish printing, 56–60
    leaf printing, 51–55
    sun printing (heliotropic), 61–65
Needlepoint canvas, 104
Neutralizer, for bleach, 114, 115
Newspaper stencils, 46–49
Noil silk, 141

O

Organza silk, 141
Oriental (indirect) printing method, 56, 58

P

Painting techniques
    fabric painting, 131
    fiber-reactive dyes, 27
    warp, 63
Paper cone, for gutta application, 144–145
Paraffin, 124, 132
Pasteur, Louis, 16
Patterns
    bleach. *See* Bleach patterns
    destructive. *See* Destructive patterns
    Nature's. *See* Nature's patterns
    repeat, 102
    sprayed, 40
    water drop. *See* Water drop patterns
    wax. *See* Wax patterns
Peel, Charlotte, 135
Perkin, William Henry, 21
Photogram process, 63–64
Photograph/photocopy transfer, 97, 105, 106
Pigment, silk painting, 150–151
Pongee silk, 17, 141
Portraits
    blind drawing, 94, 95
    child collaboration, 94, 95
    photocopy transfer, 97
    sketch, 94–95

Precut wood shapes, 134, 135, 137
Prepared-for-dyeing (PFD) fabric, 19
Presoak, in alkali, 25, 27, 76
Preval® sprayers, 46
Printing. *See also* Hand-cut stamps
    fish, 56–60
    heat-transfer, 87. *See also* Heat-transfer dyes (dispersed)
    heliotropic, 61–65
    leaf, 51–55
    moldable-foam, 66, 69–72
    sponge, 66–68
    wooden blocks, 115
Procion® H series
    liquid, 26
    overview, 24
    steaming, 28
    wax patterns, 131
Procion® MX series
    compression dyeing, 75, 76
    overview, 23–24
    steaming, 28
PROsperse dyes, 97–99
Purchasing
    cotton, 11
    fabric paints, 34
    rayon, 16
Purple dye, 21

Q

Quilts
    Blocked Energy, 135
    crazy quilt, 12
    devoré/burn-out technique, 119
    Don't Throw Away My Dolls, 71, 73
    Flying Fish Kimono quilt, 9, 57, 103
    Hollyhocks, 45
    Turquoise Blossoms, 85

R

Rain cloth, 43–44
Rayon
    acetate, 16, 88
    activating dye solution, 25
    history, 16
    purchasing, 16
    viscose, 9, 16
    washing, 18–19
Reactive dyes, 21
Ready-to-dye fabric, 19
Recipes for fiber-reactive dyes, 25
    activating dye solution, 25
    adding dyes to chemical water, 25, 26
    heat setting dyes, 25, 27–29
    preparing chemical water, 25
    thickening dyes, 25, 27
Repeat patterns, stamps, 102
Resists
    gutta. *See* Gutta resists
    stitch, 82
    wax. *See* Wax resist
Rinsing fabric
    devoré/burn-out technique, 120
    recipes, 25, 29
    stitch compression dyeing, 84
Rollagraph®, 90, 92

Rubber blocks, carving, 101,
   105–107
Rubber stamps
   block stamps, 101
   fabric-transfer ink pads, 88–89
   fish print stamps, 59, 60
   hand-cut stamps, 105–107
   MagicStamp® (PenScore ™),
      69, 71–72, 108–109
   Rollagraph®, 90, 92
Ruzich, Cheri, 43–44

S

Safety precautions
   chlorine bleach, 113
   devoré/burn-out technique, 120
   fiber-reactive dyes, 24, 29
   spray-dyeing, 47
   wax resist, 125
   wax stamping, 137
Sal soda, 27
Salt effects, silk painting, 12,
   148–149
Scheele, Carl Wilhelm, 113
Scott-Dobbins, Margaret, 32
Scrunching and dyeing
   background for hand-cut stamp
      prints, 107
   compression dyeing, 74
   procedure, 80
   water drop patterns, 46
Seals, Chinese, 60
Selective focus technique, 39
Sericulture, 13
Sharp, Lisa, 30, 42, 133
Sheet foam, for stamps, 69, 100,
   101, 103
Shibori, 74–75
Shinshi, 129, 130
Silk, 12
   activating dye solution, 25, 27
   artificial (rayon), 16
   chiffon, 79, 141
   China, 13, 58, 141
   dyeing, 80, 81
   fish print stamps, 60
   Floral Tablecloth, 17
   habotai, 58, 141, 148
   hand-cut stamp prints, 107
   Nuclear Forest #2, 18, 19
   Nuclear Forest series, 111
   Outer Space series, 126, 127, 128,
      131
   painting. See Silk painting
   Puzzle Dress, 15
   scarves, 26, 53–55
   sericulture, 13
   silkworms, 13–16
   Transformations, 14
   types, 13
   washing, 17–18
   weighting, 12
Silk painting, 9, 140
   Cows, 150
   fabric, 141
   gutta resists. See Gutta resists
   Iris Garden, 146
   Lena's Iris, 149
   Nasturtiums, 147

pigments, 150–151
   The Rose, 146
   salt effects, 12, 148–149
   techniques, 146–147
   Transformations, 140
Silkworms, 13–16
Sindelar, Margaret, 70, 90
Sketch portrait, 94–95
Soda ash, 23, 27
Sodium alginate, thickener, 27, 115
Sodium bisulfate, for devoré, 118
Sodium bisulfite, neutralizer, 114
Sodium carbonate, 23, 27
Sodium hexametaphosphate, 25, 26
Sodium thiosulfate crystals, 114
Soedarsono, Aisjah, 128
Solvent-soluble gutta (gutta serti,
   colle serti), 142–145
Space Sponge, 73
Sponge printing, 66
   animal sea sponges, 67, 68
   cellulose sponges, 67–68
   Eye Veils, 66
   Space Sponge, 73
   synthetic sponges, 68
Spray cloth, 45–48
Spray-dyeing, with newspaper stencils, 47–48
Sprayed patterns, 40
Stamps
   dragonfly, 87
   fish print, 59–60
   hand-cut. See Hand-cut stamps
   heat-transfer dye, 88, 89
   rubber. See Rubber stamps
   wax. See Wax stamping
   wheel, 90, 91
Steam setting
   canning pot steamer, 28–29
   Procion® H series, 24
   recipes, 25, 28
   salt-patterned fabrics, 149
   solvent-soluble gutta, 142
   vertical steamer, 29
   wax patterns, 131, 132
Stencils
   newspapers, 46–49
   quilting, stitch dyeing, 84–85
   spray cloth, 45
Sticky wax, 125
Stitch resist, 82
Stitching and dyeing
   Butterfly Dancers, 63
   compression dyeing, 74, 82–83
   devoré/burn-out technique, 119
   process, 83–84
   from stencils, 84–85
   Turquoise Blossoms, 85
Stock colors, 62
Stretching fabric
   canvas stretchers, 129
   devoré/burn-out technique, 120
   harite, 124, 130
   shinshi, 129, 130
Sublistatic® (sublimation printing), 87
Sun lamps, for photograms, 63
Sun printing. See Heliotropic
Supply sources, 155–156

Synthetic fabrics
   dispersed dyeing, 88
   history of dyeing, 87
   rayon. See Rayon
Synthetic sponges, 68
Synthrapol®
   rinsing agent after dyeing, 29
   scouring agent before dyeing, 17

T

Tampo (dauber), 58
Textile markers, 55, 88, 126
Thickened dye
   bleach solution, 115
   fiber-reactive dyes for compres-
      sion dyeing, 75–76
   recipes, 75
Tjanting tools (canting tool), 124,
   126, 127–128
Transferring drawing to cloth
   fabric-transfer ink pads, 88–91
   Iron-On Transfer Pens, 94–95
   mini-yardage, 89–90, 92
Tree lambs, 10
Tritik (stitch resist), 82
Twisting and dyeing, 74, 78

U

Urea pellets, 26

V

Vat dyes, 21, 62, 75
Vertical steamer, 29
Viscose rayon, 9, 16

W

Warp painting, Inkodyes, 63
Washing
   cotton, 17
   heliotropic, 65
   rayon, 18–19
   silk, 17–18
   soda, 18, 23, 27
   stitch compression dyeing, 84
Water drop patterns, 42
   Blue Norther Coat, 42, 49
   rain cloth, 43–44
   spray cloth, 45–46

spraying with newspaper stencils,
   47–48
   yardage, 49
Water softener (Calgon, Metaphos,
   sodium hexametaphosphate), 26
Water-soluble gutta, 142, 145
Watercolor techniques, 131, 146
Wax crayons, 88
Wax patterns, 122
   Galaxie Storm, 127
   Moon Sliver, 127
   Outer Space series, 126, 127, 128, 131
   planning the design, 126
   setting the dyes, 131
   Space Stream #2, 131
   wax removal, 132
   wax resist. See Wax resist
Wax resist
   batik wax, 123, 125
   beeswax, 125, 131
   Carolyn's Cows Break Loose at the Dance,
      125
   clothes dryer setting, 28
   dye painting, 123–125
   fabric painting, 131
   Inkodyes, 63
   Metamorphosis Coat, 124, 129, 132,
      133
   microcrystalline, 125
   paraffin, 124, 132
   process overview, 124
   safety, 125
   Tjanting tools, 124, 126,
      127–128
Wax stamping, 134
   Blocked Energy, 135
   Carolyn's Cows Break Loose at the Dance,
      139
   Fragments, 138
   hand-cut wood stamps, 134, 135
   making stamps, 135–136
   precut wood shapes, 134, 135, 137
   procedure, 134–139
   Turquoise Blossoms, 134
Wax transfer crayons, 93
Weighting silk, 12
Willey, Mary Ann, 76, 139
Wingate, Isabel, 141

Detail of BUTTERFLY DANCERS by Carolyn A. Dahl. (See page 63.)

Transform Fabrics
into Works of Art

Sew Any Fabric
A Quick Reference to Fabrics from A to Z
by Claire Shaeffer, Foreword by Nancy Zieman
Let your friends think you bought those satin curtains or that velvet bedspread, or share your secret — this quick reference guide for sewing the most common fabrics. Learn what thread to use, proper stitch length, and tension. If you're considering sewing new fabrics, looking for fresh ideas, or just wanting to improve your skills, you'll find this handy, easy-to-use reference is filled with practical and up-to-date information enabling you to acquire confidence, develop new skills, and improve efficiency.

Softcover • 8-1/4 x 10-7/8 • 160 pages
100 color photos, plus 50+ b&w illustrations
Item# SAFB • $23.99

The Basic Guide to Dyeing & Painting Fabric
by Cindy Walter and Jennifer Priestley
Now you can learn how to make your own one-of-a-kind hand-painted and -dyed fabrics with this exciting new book! You'll find 20 techniques for dyeing and painting wearables, accessories, and home décor. Also features more than 6 projects, including a vest, scarf, quilts, and pillows, along with step-by-step instructions. You'll love how these easy techniques will brighten up your life!

Softcover • 8-1/4 x 10-7/8 • 96 pages
200 color photos
Item# FTDF • $19.99

Creating Texture with Textiles!
by Linda McGehee
Written for all levels of sewers, this user-friendly guide features step-by-step instructions to create spectacular one-of-a-kind designs on fabric with the use of any sewing machine. Techniques include piecing, spiraling, appliqué, piping, cording, embroidery, beading, among others.

Softcover • 8-1/4 x 10-7/8 • 128 pages
200 color photos and 20 illustrations
Item# TWT • $21.95

African Fabrics
Sewing Contemporary Fashion With Ethnic Flair
by Ronke Luke-Boone
Author and designer Ronke Luke-Boone tells you where to buy fabrics, how to choose the right ones, and the best techniques for sewing them. Besides covering the six most popular African fabrics, this guide will show you how they are produced and ways to incorporate them into contemporary designs for men, women, and children, as well as home décor. Offers 14 original projects, including a tote bag, tunic, and pillows, four of which have full-size patterns.

Softcover • 8-1/4 x 10-7/8 • 144 pages
80 illustrations • 200 color photos
Item# AFRIF • $22.95

Art to Wear with Asian Flair
by Stephanie Masae Kimura
Liven up your wardrobe with cheerful colors, whimsical lines and the comfortable shapes of author Stephanie Kimura's designs. Learn to design original garments, lush with Asian flair with the 22 Asian motif templates such as a golden dragon, Geisha, crane, lotus, pagoda, peony and chrysanthemum. Includes easy-to-follow instructions for designing and embellishing each of the 5 projects — a purse, vest, two jackets and a kimono.

Softcover • 8-1/4 x 10-7/8 • 128 pages
250+ color photos
Item# AWAF • $23.95

The Art of Manipulating Fabric
by Colette Wolff
Presenting an encyclopedia of techniques to resurface, reshape, restructure, and reconstruct fabric. More than 350 diagrams will show you how to begin with the simplest flat piece of cloth and progress to a beautiful finished tapestry.

Softcover • 8-1/4 x 10-7/8
320 pages • illustrations throughout
Item# AOMF • $29.95